An American Family

An American Family

by NATALIE ROTHSTEIN

Natalie Rothstein

FITHIAN PRESS · SANTA BARBARA, CA · 1999

ACKNOWLEDGMENTS

This book is a hybrid. Part history, part memoir, it tells the story of the immigrant experience through three generations of my family. I want to thank those who have helped me in telling that story.

I am very grateful for the research centers available in the Boston area and for the assistance provided by their personnel. These include the American Jewish Historical Society, Brandeis University Library, the Hebrew College Library, and the New England branch of the National Archives.

In addition, I am grateful to be a member of the Jewish Genealogical Society of Greater Boston. The society is an invaluable resource for anyone embarked on the often-elusive search for family. It provides information, direction, and a network of connections.

My gratitude and appreciation to Boris Borisov of Vilnius and Oleg Magaril of Minsk for making my journey to the past unforgettable.

Special thanks go to Ina Friedman, Thelma Gruenbaum, and Roberta Winston, my Writing Group colleagues, for their support, encouragement and wise counsel. Also to Gail Stein, whose thoughtful reading of the manuscript and incisive comments were of enormous help.

And to my husband, Alan, who makes all things possible, my everlasting love.

Copyright © 1999 by Natalie Rothstein
All rights reserved
Printed in the United States of America

A portion of the text first appeared in the Fall 1998 issue of *The Reporter*
Cover map from *Atlas of Jewish History* by Martin Gilbert, Routledge.

Published by Fithian Press
A division of Daniel and Daniel, Publishers, Inc.
Post Office Box 1525
Santa Barbara, CA 93102

LIBRARY OF CONGRESS CATALOGING-IN-PUBLICATION DATA
Rothstein, Natalie, (date)
    An American family / by Natalie Rothstein.
        p.   cm.
    Includes bibliographical references
    ISBN 1-56474-280-6 (alk. paper)
    1. Rothstein, Natalie, (date). 2. Jews—Massachusetts—Boston—Biography. 3. Jews, Russian—Massachusetts—Boston—Biography. 4. Immigrants—Massachusetts—Boston—Biography. 5. Frumkin family. 6. Boston (Mass.)—Biography.   I. Title.
F73.9.J5R67 1999
974.4'61'004924'0092
[B]—dc21   98-30618
                                                          CIP

This book is dedicated with love and honor to the memory of my parents,
Frances and Frank Manson,
and my grandparents,
Anne and Harris Manson, and Jennie and William Franklin

and to
my beloved children, Peter, Steven and Katie,
and my adored grandchildren, Megan, Jessye, Galen, Isaac, Leah, and Adam
whose lives are the continuing chapters
in the story of an American family

Contents

FRUMKIN (FRANKLIN) FAMILY

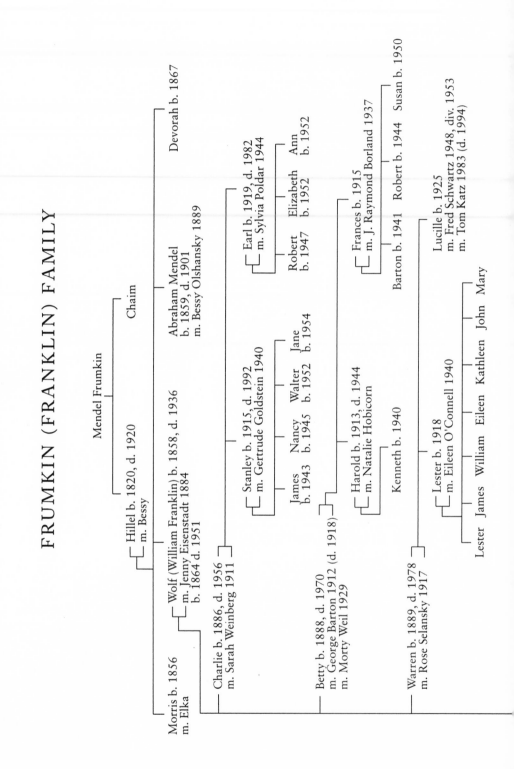

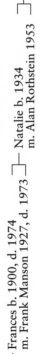

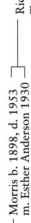

George b. 1896, d. 1973
m. Ethel Selansky 1919, div. 1926
m. Lena Kumins 1928

Morris b. 1898, d. 1953
m. Esther Anderson 1930

Richard b. 1930
m. Naomi Cohen 1952, div. 1957
m. Ilse Bruningen

Sergei b. 1959
Anna b. 1966

Frances b. 1900, d. 1974
m. Frank Manson 1927, d. 1973

Natalie b. 1934
m. Alan Rothstein 1953

Peter b. 1954
m. Mary Crowe 1980, div. 1987

Megan b. 1981
Jessye b. 1983

Steven b. 1956
m. Susan Maze 1987

Galen Maze b. 1980
Isaac b. 1990

Katie b. 1960
m. David Paikin 1983

Leah b.1988
Adam b. 1990

Frank b. 1902, d. 1971
m. Betty Levenson 1923, div. 1933
m. Clara Carlson 1935

Bessie b. 1904, d. 1991
m. Samuel Kraft 1928

Doris b. 1931
m. Ted Goodman 1951

Billy b. 1958
Andy b. 1961

Arthur b. 1906, d. 1979
m. Augusta Cantor 1931

Helen b. 1908, d. 1982
m. Moses Parker 1931

Janet b. 1935
m. Irwin Freedman 1955

Laura b. 1957
Patty b. 1958
Jennifer b. 1962
Ken b. 1978

Deborah b. 1945
m. Ken Solnit 1970

Matthew b. 1978
Jonathan b. 1981

MOVSCHOVITZ (MANSON) FAMILY

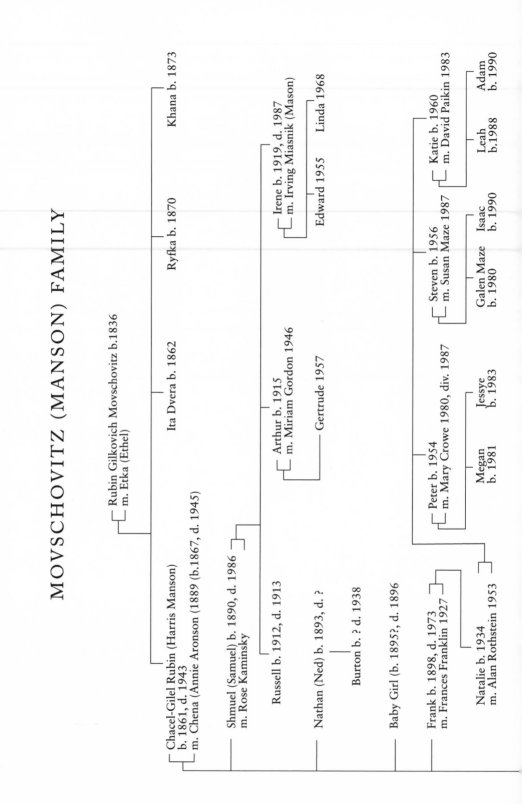

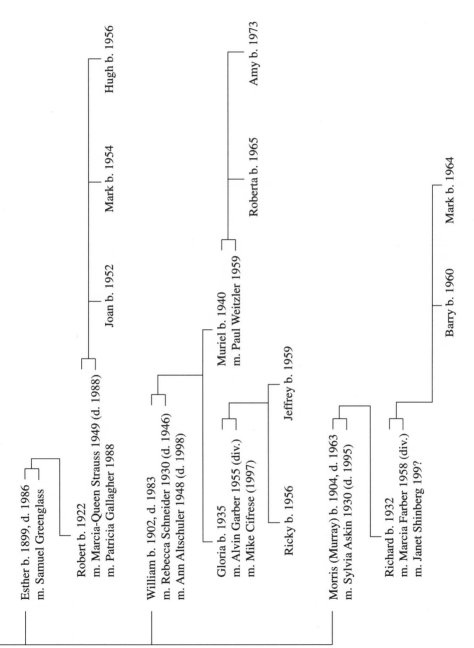

Esther b. 1899, d. 1986
m. Samuel Greenglass

Robert b. 1922
m. Marcia-Queen Strauss 1949 (d. 1988)
m. Patricia Gallagher 1988

Joan b. 1952

Mark b. 1954

Hugh b. 1956

William b. 1902, d. 1983
m. Rebecca Schneider 1930 (d. 1946)
m. Ann Altschuler 1948 (d. 1998)

Gloria b. 1935
m. Alvin Garber 1955 (div.)
m. Mike Cifrese (1997)

Muriel b. 1940
m. Paul Weitzler 1959

Roberta b. 1965

Amy b. 1973

Ricky b. 1956

Jeffrey b. 1959

Morris (Murray) b. 1904, d. 1963
m. Sylvia Askin 1930 (d. 1995)

Richard b. 1932
m. Marcia Farber 1958 (div.)
m. Janet Shinberg 199?

Barry b. 1960

Mark b. 1964

Preface

Remember the days of old, consider the years of many generations; ask thy [mo]ther and [s]he will show thee, thy elders and they will tell thee.

—*Deuteronomy 32:7*

"WHERE DO I COME FROM?" It's a question all children ask at one time or another. But when my then ten-year-old granddaughter, Megan, asked it of me, I knew that she was not seeking the answer in any biological context. She has known where babies come from almost from the time she herself was a baby. As a two-year-old she was present, as was I, at the home-birth of her sister, our beloved Jessye.

I discounted the possibility that Megan could be asking about her geographical origins. She has lived her entire life in one place. But the thought did put me in mind of the old joke.

"Where do I come from?" asks Billy. Whereupon his mother launches into a long, rambling and eventually brain-numbing discourse on "how babies are born." "Oh," says Billy, "I just wondered because Timmy comes from Pittsburgh."

No, Megan was inquiring about neither biology nor geography. She was asking about her roots and her history. She wanted to know from whom she was descended. Who were her people? And so, as grandmothers will do with adored grandchildren, I tried my best to answer her. Only I don't think my best was quite good enough.

Oh, I told her stories about the past, about my parents and how they had met at a wedding. I told her that my mother had been one of ten children and that my Aunt Helen, the youngest of the ten, had slept in a bureau drawer as an infant, the only sleeping space available in an overcrowded household.

I told Megan the little I knew about my grandparents: how they had come from the "old country" to start a new life of freedom in America. It was the ordinary immigrant story. But even as I spoke, I knew that there was nothing "ordinary" about people who lived that extraordinary experience, people who left their homes, their families, and their countries to face unknown hardships in a new land. I knew it was the saga and the glory of America.

It seemed very clear that a few sketchy stories could not begin to tell Megan where she came from. Something more was required. That something more is this book.

I have read books about immigrants, about the old country and the new world. I am collecting old photos and have spent more time than I would have imagined in archives and libraries.

I became fully absorbed in this project while Megan, as life and time would have it, has moved on to other things. She plays soccer, she goes to the mall, she is a teenager. It may be that like the apocryphal Billy and his friend from Pittsburgh, Megan merely wanted some basic facts. And like Billy's mom, I may be guilty of overdoing it.

Yet somehow I don't think so. Rooting about in one's roots seems to me a perfectly reasonable thing to do. The past is a legacy, connecting us through the strands of time to our history and linking us to the future. Surely, for those who ask "Where do I come from?" it's nice to go in search of one's own personal Pittsburgh.

An American Family

Prologue

There is a time to love and a time to hate,
A time to rejoice and a time to weep.

—*Ecclessiastes*

IT WAS A JOURNEY to the past as well as a journey home, to a place I had never been. Two thirds of my way through this book I had come to Belarus in search of my roots, even though I knew that there was very little chance of finding anything there.

Pogroms, emigration, and then the Holocaust had obliterated the Jewish population of Eastern Europe. Nine out of every ten Jews had been murdered in World War II, and all that remains today are a relative handful of people and a few plaques and monuments of stone, remnants of a once vital community.

Yet there I was, Wolf Frumkin's American granddaughter, returning to the village in old Russia, to the home he left behind more than one hundred years ago.

This was the "old country." And indeed, except for the occasional television antenna sprouting on the roof of a peasant home, this small village of Korzangorodok, fifty miles east of Pinsk, still looks very much like a place that time has forgotten.

Korzangorodok is dirt roads, wooden houses, and horse-drawn wagons. It is a white church topped with yellow onion domes. It is a village of 3,000 people whose dark, rough clothing and black rubber boots betray their provincial background.

The trip to Korzangorodok began with a three-hour drive south from the capital, Minsk. But the genesis of this journey, in fact, was long ago. The tracing of my family tree had developed from a casual hobby to a

17

serious search. I had spent untold hours exploring records and archives, and while some of my efforts had met with resounding success, others had not.

Searching for my grandparents' names, I had become proficient in the ways of microfilm and microfiche. I had scoured census and naturalization records and old city directories. In the 1900 census I had found my mother listed as an infant, the newest member of the Frumkin household. But I was still trying to find the name of the ship and the port of entry that had brought my ancestors to the New World.

One of the most important sources of family history was, alas, no longer available to me: my family. My mother, one of ten children, was gone, as were all her siblings. Now there was no one to talk to, no oral histories to take, only a paper trail to follow.

Acutely aware that my late-developing interest in family history was, in this instance, too late, I was chastened and saddened by the stories untold, the tales unknown, the links missing from a long chain.

Upon our arrival in Korzangorodok, we set about meeting people through our guide, Oleg, an energetic and vigorous young teacher. I had asked him to help us find the oldest citizens in town, the people with the longest memories, who might be willing to talk to us.

Arriving at the town hall, Oleg darted inside, returning shortly with the mayor in tow. He was a man of about forty-five, and he eagerly volunteered to join us. His seventy-six-year-old mother would surely want to talk to us, he said, but first he insisted on a little tour.

We stood in a nearly empty field, staring at a picket fence surrounding a small one-story wooden house, a simple, ordinary scene endlessly repeated throughout the village. This, said the mayor, was the former site of the synagogue and the school.

Next he led us to a large recessed area of overgrown brush, surrounded by earthen embankments. Once this had been the Jewish cemetery. Here Wolf's parents, my great-grandparents, Hillel and Bessy, most surely were buried.

Yet nothing exists here any longer—no markers, no tombstones. All that remains is the long grass and brambles of a deserted patch of land. It is a desecrated wasteland. Century-old family headstones have disappeared, carted away during the war to be used as paving stones.

Family documents had already established Korzangorodok as my ancestral village. And now Oleg's resourcefulness had turned up corroborating records in the archives in Minsk.

Entitled "Family History of Korzangorodok, Jewish community of Pinsk District in Minsk Province," and dated 1905, the records indicated, said Oleg, that "there were many Frumkins in Korzangorodok then."

The document shows that in 1905 my great-grandfather Hillel was still living; his sons, Mendel and Morris, were there too.

Though I knew that my grandfather Wolf had two brothers, the archives also record a sister, Devorah. So it would seem that my mother had an aunt of whose existence—and fate—we know nothing.

My own research had taught me that Korzangorodok had been a Jewish community since the sixteenth century and that the Jewish population in 1897, a few years after my grandparents left, had been 1,597 or forty-eight percent. Then it was a *shtetl*, a small Russian village with a Jewish community. Today it is still a village, but no longer a *shtetl*. No Jews remain. The wooden synagogue that once stood at the center of the village is gone; the school and the cemetery are also gone, silent echoes of the past.

How many of Korzangorodok's Jews survived World War II is not known. But in a mass grave lie 937 of those who did not survive.

We learned how it happened during our visit with the mayor's mother. Invited into her home, we were ushered into the kitchen, where her husband sat alone at the table, eating his midday meal, neither acknowledging our presence nor participating in any discussion.

A long, dark skirt, heavy sweater and stockings, and a *babushka* (scarf) defined the tiny, elderly woman. The mother of nine children, she showed me the black-bordered photograph of her fifty-two-year-old son who had died the previous year. Clearly unaccustomed to guests, she fluttered about her kitchen offering us chairs, a drink, fried eggs.

Through Oleg she spoke of events that had taken place more than half a century ago as if they had occurred only yesterday.

"The central part of the *shtetl* was all Jewish," she said. "They were merchants and traders; there were a lot of stores here...

"The war began the first of September 1939. The Germans came here in 1941 after their invasion. First they made a ghetto, then after creating the ghetto, in 1942, they shot everybody. At once. In one moment...

"We were very afraid because these were our neighbors. The Nazis made a hole [a ditch] and then another hole. And the people thought, after the Jews, we would be next...."

No one spoke. It was the kind of silence in which all you hear is the sound of your own heart beat. A few weak rays of late afternoon sun slanted through the single window, and I stared at the particles of dust dancing fitfully in the air.

I asked our hostess about my family. Did she remember any Frumkins? Or Eisenstadts, my grandmother's people? No, she did not recognize those names, but she reached out and opened a little drawer in the kitchen table and extracted a piece of paper.

It was a list. When she started to read we were stunned. All these years—was it possible?—she had kept this list in a kitchen drawer. She had not put it away with important papers; she had not destroyed it; she had kept it close by in the place where she ate her daily meals, where her husband, his fork scraping at his metal dish, continued eating his solitary meal.

The list was an inventory of names, family names of her former Jewish neighbors. We listened with ineffable sadness to a roster of the doomed, those who had been executed. Saperstein, Kusicovich, Latinsky, Isaacs.... These were some of the 937 Jew of Korzangorodok who are remembered and are marked at a memorial site.

Heavy black chains isolate a stretch of wooded glen. Within, a stone monument bears the names of the dead. The silence is disquieting, eerie.

I tried to read the names. Oleg helped me search for Frumkins, for Eisenstadts. But they were not listed. Some of my family, we know, did escape annihilation, while others perished in the war—where and when, we don't know.

I know I have cousins who survived the war; today they live in Moscow and Israel. They were lucky. Those like my grandparents, who fled the terror and oppression of an earlier time, were even more fortunate. They were among the more than two million Jews who swarmed to the *Goldene Medina*, the Golden Land, America, creating the Great Migration of 1881 to 1914.

That search for a better life is what drove Wolf Frumkin out of Korzangorodok sometime around 1889. He and my grandmother Jennie had been married eight years and had three children. With only enough money for a single passage, Wolf left for America alone. Five years later, in 1894, his family was reunited when Jennie and the children joined him in Boston.

My grandmother lived on until 1951, but my grandfather died in 1936, when I was only two years old. A recent visit to the cemetery and his tombstone told me something I never knew—his Hebrew name was Isaac, the same as my youngest grandson.

I don't know what genes little Isaac may have inherited from his great-great-grandfather. Is there a gene for music? Will he play the violin as Wolf Frumkin did? Will he be good with his hands, a master carpenter as was my grandfather? I don't know.

What I do know is that Isaac, his cousins, and indeed all of us are heirs to the legacy that Wolf and Jennie Frumkin bequeathed us. Their story was one of struggle and they made our story, that of an American family, possible.

1. The Old World

Whoever teaches [her child] reaches not alone [her child] but also [her child's child] and so on to the end of generations.

—*The Talmud*

I remember my Grandpa Manson. An old man when I knew him, he sat at the kitchen table in the first floor apartment he shared with my grandmother in a three-decker building, on Intervale Street. They lived in Roxbury, a predominantly Jewish neighborhood of Boston. On Sundays my father would bring me to visit his parents and, while Grandma fussed with me, patting my cheek, smoothing my hair, Grandpa remained quiet, remote and apart.

Grandma was built like a round pudding cake, had a twinkle in her eye and chattered nonstop. I would frequently have to look to my father for help in understanding her conversation, since it was peppered with Yiddish—although it is more likely that the difficulty lay in the fact that her Yiddish was sprinkled with occasional phrases of English.

Grandpa spoke Yiddish too—that is, on the rare occasions when he spoke at all. (I was used to that funny-sounding guttural language, but that didn't mean I understood it. It was what my parents spoke when they didn't want me to know what they were discussing. "Little pitchers have big ears," they would say as they lapsed into Yiddish.) Why, I would ask my father, why doesn't Grandpa talk? Because, I was told, he doesn't hear very well anymore. He had grown deaf in his old age and had retreated into a private world of silence and memories. While Grandma was insisting that I have some pastry, some fruit, that I "eat, eat," Grandpa, small and thin, would sit in unapproachable silence.

He died in 1943 when I was nine years old.

Thinking back on the somewhat distant figure he presented to me, I would have trouble associating my white-haired grandfather with the dark-bearded young man who, fifty years earlier, had posed proudly for his photograph with his family. Wearing the traditional frock coat and derby hat of the Orthodox Jew (a style of dress that would be shed in the New World), Harris Movschovitz stood with his wife, Annie, as they flank his mother, Ethel, who was holding baby Shmuel, my father's brother and Harris and Annie's first-born. The year is 1890.

What dreams they must have had then as a young family starting out. Surely they heard the tales about America that had become common among all the other Jews living in the Pale. They must have read the letters and marveled that in the New World "cobbler and teacher have the same title—Mister—and all the children, boys and girls, Jews and Gentiles, go to school!"*

Once those dreams caught hold of you, they grew and fed on the imagination. Just think, in America there was no czar, nobody to tell you that you could not live here or you could not work there. Why, in America it was possible through hard work to own your own business, perhaps even a home of your own.

Letters from America spelled out the content of their dreams. Those who could read, did; those who couldn't, listened.

There were two basic languages of the *shtetl*: Hebrew and Yiddish. Hebrew, taught in the *cheder*, the school, was the language of study. Yiddish was the *"mama-loshen,"* the mother tongue spoken by millions of Jews in Eastern Europe for a thousand years. Russian might be learned from a university student, perhaps in exchange for hot meals.

Girls like my Grandmother Annie would not have learned Hebrew. To go to *cheder* in order to study the Talmud and Torah was only for boys. Girls were taught housework; boys were taught the Book. Both learned very early what their proper places were in the scheme of things.

Annie spoke Yiddish, the language of the ghetto. It contained bits of German, Russian and Polish, as well as Hebrew, the Jewish language of prayer. Whatever country they came from, the Jews of Eastern Europe all spoke Yiddish.

I don't know if my grandmother could read Yiddish. I do know that she never learned to read or write English. In 1913, her mark of "x" is what passed for her written assent on the Commonwealth of Massachusetts documents changing the name of Harris Manschowitz [sic] to that of Harris Manson.

---

*Meltzer, Milton. *Remember the Days.*

In America one could be an individual. In the nineteenth-century *shtetl* life of the Jew, people were defined by their Jewishness. It didn't matter if they were observant Jews or not. It didn't matter if they lit the candles to welcome the Sabbath or if they espoused heretical, atheistic ideas. Gertrude Stein's famed description of a rose could be applied equally to her people with no loss of meaning: A Jew is a Jew is a Jew is a Jew.

A Jew was also a Litvak or Galitzianer, designations applied by one Jewish group to another and not meant to be interpreted as terms of endearment. "Humph, a Litvak. I should have known; no sense of humor," someone from Galicia might say. And a Lithuanian Jew, or Litvak, barely able to conceal his contempt for a Galitzianer, would label him as fanatic, a *"meshuggener."*

That there were differences between Litvaks and Galitzianers is indisputable. For the Litvaks, knowledge and learning were essential. But in Galicia the Hassidic movement flourished, a movement created in the mid-eighteenth century by Israel ben Eliezer. Known as the Baal Shem Tov or the Master of the Good Name, he rebelled against the excessive intellectualism of the Lithuanian Jews and taught that the heart, not the head, was where the true love of God would be found. Dance, song and joyous worship were all encouraged under Hassidism.

In the *shtetl*, life for men and women was clearly defined. A man might work as a tailor or baker, a cobbler or carpenter. In the home, the father enjoyed the respect of his family.

There is an old adage used to describe the labors of a housewife. "Man labors from sun to sun, but woman's work is never done." Those words were never more fitting than when applied to the Jewish housewife of the *shtetl*. And for women married to Orthodox Jewish men, there was the added burden of taking on the menial labor while her husband had the "higher calling" and privilege of studying and praying in the *shul* all day.

These women "had to chop wood for the oven, bake the bread, go considerable distances to draw water from some well, and carry it uphill even when the streets were covered with slippery ice. Worst of all, underwear, linen sheets, tablecloths, and the like, had to be washed in the river nearly a mile away, even in the wintry months when the washing had to be done through a hole in the ice...."* All of this had to be endured along with the routine housework and the bearing and rearing of children.

---

*Howe and Libo. *How We Lived.* p. 7.

In addition to all the domestic chores required of women, they often had other work as well. They were pretzel-makers and sausage-makers. They were bathhouse attendants and pickle-sellers. and what would *shtetl* life have been without the presence of the matchmaker? There could be no more important job than bringing together a man and a woman in marriage. Such a crucial matter could not be left to chance; it required the careful intercession of a guiding hand.

Most of us have an image of what life was like in those small Eastern European villages. We've read the stories; we've seen the movies. Visions depicted in drawings and paintings further feed our imagination. The Russian Jewish existence has had no better interpreter than artist Marc Chagall. He lived the life. And then, through the genius of his art, he recreated it. Chagall gave us pictures of peasant towns where people, in fanciful and dream-like visions, might escape the harshness of life simply by floating above it. Surely, rising above it all is a symbol of survival—and hope.

We can only speculate how much hope might have existed among the people of the *shtetl*. For the most part, their lives consisted of privation and persecution. They lived in ghettos, their freedom to settle or even to travel severely limited.

Ironically, the very isolation enforced upon the Jews may have given them strength, community and a cohesive sense of identity. In other words, the world of the ghetto—segregated, onerous and difficult—probably helped solidify the bonds of Jewish life through the centuries. A further irony, of course, is that the freedom enjoyed by the modern American Jew may be contributing to the assimilation, intermarriage and loss of *Yiddishkeit*, or Jewishness. It's harder to know who you are if you can be anything you want; the Eastern European *shtetl* Jew had no such problem.

There was a small elite among the Russian Jewish population, and they lived a life of some privilege. The intellectual, often-rich elite of the Russian Jews numbered perhaps 300,000. They were permitted to live outside the Pale. They might be artisans practicing their trades or merchants and businessmen for whom travel across borders was allowed. Few, however, achieved the renown the Rothschild family did in their roles as counselors and bankers to kings.

As for the rest? About 1.7 million Jews lived in the urban centers of Russian-held Poland, while almost 5 million Jews—half the world's Jewish population—lived in city ghettos or in villages and towns throughout the Pale. It was especially in those towns and villages—the *shtetlach*—that the misery of life bore down on the people. They were poor and they were persecuted. And they were made to suffer for their religion.

Russia followed a feudal system in which millions of people lived as serfs, virtual slaves. They were indentured to the land; whoever owned the land, in effect, owned them. Their labor and their efforts all accrued to the landowner. These serfs, like the Jews, were victims of a crude system, but they were not subject to the additional brutalities suffered by the Jews. A lifetime of conscription into the czar's army or the loss of life or property in a pogrom, those terrors were exclusive to Jews.

But everyone knew that things like that did not happen in America.

11. Life in the Pale

AMERICA. Everywhere throughout Mother Russia, in the *shtetlach* and towns, in the marketplace and city square, Jews talked of the new country. Harris and Annie Movschovitz heard the talk; so did Wolf and Jennie Frumkin. Only the most naive believed that in America the streets were truly paved with gold. But you didn't have to believe in fairy tales to know that a person could live free and without fear in the New World.

So it was that in 1889 my Grandfather Wolf Frumkin, age thirty-one, a carpenter from Korzangorodok in the Russian province of Belarus, said goodbye to his wife, Jennie, and their three small children and began the long journey to America. And in 1892, propelled by the same dream, my paternal grandparents, Harris, age thirty-one, and Chana or Anna Movschovitz, age twenty-five, left Rumsiskes in Lithuania with their two-year-old son, Shmuel.

They left all that was known, all that was familiar, in exchange for the anxious hope that life in America could be better.

The emigration of my grandparents was emblematic of the two million Eastern European Jews who fled their homelands to come to America. They were part of what was known as the Great Migration during the years 1880 to 1914.

Ninety percent of these Eastern European Jews emigrated to America. The rest dispersed to various countries, many to Palestine. That ancient land of the Bible was a magnet for the impassioned reformers and believers in Zionism. As a social and political movement, Zionism attracted many intellectual Jews who had been radicalized by the conditions under which they lived. Their dream of a homeland, of a Jewish state, would be realized in 1948 with the establishment of the state of Israel.

Wolf and Jennie and Harris and Annie, like the majority of their countrymen, were not intellectuals. They were poor and they were Jews, and in the latter half of the nineteenth century there was not much future in Russia for such people.

Cholera and famine killed thousands. Pogroms terrorized and killed more as the czar's police, the dreaded Cossacks, swooped down on villages, leaving devastation in their wake. And for a Jewish boy, being drafted into the army was another menace, a living death.

To a Jew, compulsory military service meant more than the normal twenty-five years of service. If the poor, unfortunate boy was drafted, he either ran away, hid or injured himself—lopping off a finger with a knife was one route for those who would avoid the draft. When all these efforts failed and the hapless youth was taken off to the army, his family sat *shiva*, the Jewish custom of mourning the dead. It was as if they would never see their son or brother again. In many cases, they never did.

At age nineteen Harris Movschovitz was drafted into the local unit of the National Guard. How long he served or even if he served is not known. But it is clear that, at some point, he escaped. Perhaps unable to go back to his home in Yanova, he stayed in the *shtetl* of Rumsiskes (Rumshishok) close by, where he met and married Chana Aronzen, daughter of Shmuel-Josel and Ida Jacobson Aronzen.

Despite his untenable situation and fear of discovery, Harris, the only son of Rueben and Etka (Ethel), nevertheless slipped back and forth to Yanova to see his parents and three younger sisters. Perhaps the only way to ease his desperate circumstances was to do what so many were doing: flee. To America. More and more, for Harris and Wolf and the Jews of Eastern Europe, the future—and freedom—belonged to America.

Life for Russian Jews was severely limited. Always there was the fear of disease, the draft, and pogroms. And since 1882, when the notorious May Laws were instituted, things had gotten even worse.

In 1881, on a Sunday in March, as Czar Alexander II rode in his

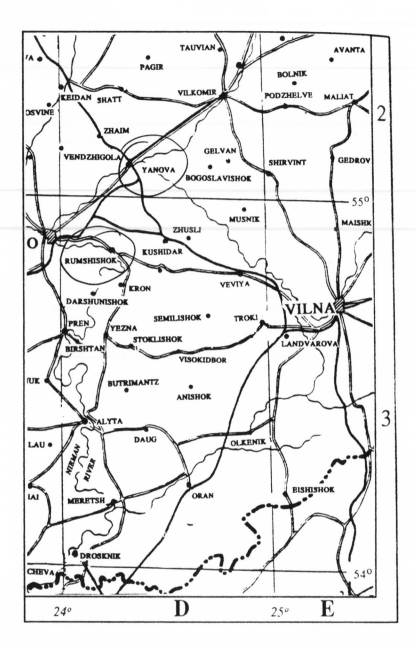

FROM *LITHUANIAN JEWISH COMMUNITIES* BY NANCY AND STUART
SCHOENBERG, GARLAND PUBLISHING, INC., 1991

sleigh along the Catherine Canal in St. Petersburg, a man belonging to a revolutionary terrorist group hurled a bomb at him. It was the seventh assassination attempt on the czar by a group calling itself The People's Will. This time they succeeded. Both the czar and his assassin died instantly.

In the words of the Prime Minister of Britain, Benjamin Disreali—himself a Jew—Alexander II had been "the kindliest prince who ever ruled Russia," a reference to the czar's reign being characterized by sweeping reforms and liberalization of policy.

A major achievement of Alexander's rule was the emancipation of serfs. Thirty million of these serfs, or slaves, were freed. And for Russian Jews, there would also be new freedoms under the "Czar Liberator."

Alexander II abolished juvenile conscription, a heinous practice that had been instituted under the despotic reign of Czar Nicholas (1825–1855). Under Nicholas, the "Iron Czar," Jewish boys were taken from their families at age twelve and sent to military posts for six years. Then at eighteen, they were subject to the regular twenty-five-year military service to which non-Jews were also liable. The purpose of these tyrannical czarist rules was to force conversion and assimilation of Jews. The draft quota was high during the reign of Nicholas, but not as high as the fear and fury of the Jewish community.

It was Nicholas who, in 1851, established the "Temporary Rules Concerning the Assortment of Jews," in which the Jewish population of Russia was divided into five classes: guild merchants, petty traders, artisans, laborers, and unemployed idlers. No other occupations were open to Russia's Jews.

In addition to freeing the "soldier" children, Alexander instituted other reforms that benefited Russia's Jews. Schools and universities were again opened to Jews; some Jewish merchants were allowed to travel or move, to leave the Pale, the area where most of Russia's Jews were confined.

The enclosed district known as the Pale of Settlement was created under the reign of Catherine the Great in 1791. After three successive partitions of Poland occurred, bringing upwards of a million Polish Jews into the Russian fold, the czarina was convinced that these illiterate ghetto Jews were not beneficial to her empire. By creating the Pale, she would isolate them, keep them apart from true Russians.

The Pale covered an area from the Baltic Sea to the Black Sea and was about the size of Texas. Almost five million Jews lived there, 94 percent of the total Jewish population of Russia.

Forced to live in the Pale, Russian Jews' lives were often desperate

The Pale, 1835–1917

struggles to survive. The majority of Jews in the Pale lived in abject poverty, persecuted and oppressed. There were predators of all kinds. The forests surrounding the *shtetlach* swarmed with wolves who prowled the night, and the Cossacks were of equal danger. More than once did the czar's police consume too much vodka, spurring riotous evenings of breaking up a few Jewish homes and perhaps a few Jewish bones as well.

But the Jews of Eastern Europe somehow survived. More than survive, they endured. Descendants of Abraham, of a tribal, nomadic people living in the Middle East, Jews can trace their history back to 2,000 years before Christ. Known as Israelites, Jews suffered the destruction of Jerusalem in A.D. 70, when the Romans conquered Palestine. This began the Diaspora, the dispersal of Jews to all parts of the world, where their existence has so often been precarious.

In Russia, Jews learned that if they could not go to the czar's schools, they would have their own schools. Whether in villages or towns, their workaday lives and their daily struggles displayed a devotion to work, to study, and to maintaining their faith. In every *shtetl* there was a synagogue. And every Jewish family in every *shtetl*, no matter if they ate only potatoes all week, sat down on the Sabbath to a table lit by candles and graced with food for the Shabbas meal.

It was astonishing that out of this world of Russian Jews, a world of limitations, came scholars and writers and philosophers and, yes, carpenters and cigar-makers. Their survival is a testament to the human spirit. But these were real people, not romantic images, people whose endurance was heroic, but whose daily lives were not. They were like all people; they could be petty or jealous or angry. And they could laugh at themselves, even at their misfortunes.

They could make jokes about their misery and poverty. An old Yiddish proverb says *"Shver tsu zayn a Yid,"* "It is hard to be a Jew." Yet, almost as a source of pride or one-upmanship, if you will, Jews might lament, even exaggerate, their condition. Relating how poor the homes were in their *shtetl*, one man says, "Zosleh was so poor that there was no glass for the windows."

"So, who had windows?"

"Who said windows? A board fell over, so there was a hole, a window."

So it was that in 1881 Jews in Russia lived and struggled and married, had children and died. Only more of them began dying in 1881.

With the assassination of Alexander II the days of benevolent rule for Russia and her Jews were at an end. For now it was Alexander's son, the brutal Alexander III, who reigned as czar of all Russia. And this czar, who had disapproved of his lenient father and his reforms, this czar would not show such weakness toward Jews. This czar hated Jews.

Pogroms and riots broke out throughout the land. Thousands of Jews were killed or injured. And in May of 1882, new laws were enacted denying Jews even the most rudimentary of freedoms.

There were over "six hundred fifty restrictive laws in force against the Jews. Jews were barred from owning or renting land outside the towns or cities...Quotas were set to keep Jews out of schools and universities. Jews could not practice law or take part in local elections...Jews [previously] allowed to live in the big cities outside the Pale...were abruptly cast out.... Their liquor trade was made a government monopoly and thousands of Jews running inns and restaurants lost their livelihoods."*

Before the May Laws, Jews could move from one town to another in the Pale. Now it was forbidden. As a result of pogroms and the "Temporary Orders Concerning the Jews" (orders which remained in effect until the Russian Revolution of 1917), Jews in the towns and villages began to realize that life as they had known it had become even more impossible.

In 1882, my grandmother, Jennie Eisenstadt [or Isenstein], age eighteen, daughter of Louis and Fredl, was about to marry Wolf Frumkin, age twenty-four, son of Hillel and Bessy. Perhaps one always needs courage to join one's destiny with that of another; to do so in that fateful year of 1882 one had to be particularly young and brave.

Like Sholom Aleichem's Tevya, Jews throughout Mother Russia's Anatevkas knew, indeed, that it was *"shver tsu sayn a Yid"*—hard to be a Jew.

---

*Metzler, Milton. *Remember the Days*. p. 33.

III. The Shtetl

No government has ever succeeded in making everyone equally happy. Too many governments have succeeded in making everyone equally miserable.

—*Bernard Baruch*

THE FIRST JEWS to settle in America came in 1654 by way of Brazil and Holland after being expelled from Spain in 1492. Refugees from the Spanish Inquisition, they were only twenty-three in number. Today American Jews, 5.5 million strong, comprise the largest Jewish community in the world, half a million more than those who live in Israel.

Sephardic Jews, those of Spanish or Portuguese origin, were the first to settle in America, and their numbers increased in the seventeenth and eighteenth centuries. The Touro Synagogue in Newport, Rhode Island, established in 1763, remains today as a historic landmark as well as an active congregation.

Then came the Ashkenazi Jews, those with origins in Western and Eastern Europe. The next wave of immigration took place in the eighteenth century, when the German Jews came. Most present-day American Jews, however, can trace their ancestors to the Great Migration. The largest number of those Jewish immigrants came from what was then Russia. These were our people.

Some of the new immigrants came from large cities such as Kiev or Vilna, but most of them came from small towns and villages. They were young and old, and mostly poor. They were cobblers and tailors, fishmongers and merchants.

Wolf Frumkin left more than his wife, Jennie, and their three children when he left Russia. He left behind his parents, Hillel and Bessy, his brothers, Morris and Abraham, and a sister, Devorah. Only Morris would eventually follow his brother to Boston.

The Frumkins were carpenters and builders. And musicians. My great-grandfather made violins, and all of his children played the instrument. By my mother's generation, the musical genes had been somewhat dissipated. As a girl, my mother played the piano. But we never had a piano in our apartment. Either we didn't have the room, or we didn't have the money. Whatever the reason, I know she missed it. All of her life she kept her old sheet music, yellowed and torn, in a bureau drawer.

Mother's sister, Bessie, was musical too. But unlike my mother, who was quiet and contemplative, Bessie was too impatient for piano lessons. She had a big voice and a big personality to go with it. She bore a certain resemblance to her show-business idol, the self-styled "Last of the Red-Hot Mamas," Sophie Tucker. I used to get goose flesh listening to Aunt Bessie belt out Tucker's signature song, "Some of These Days."

Back in Korzangorodok, music must have been a welcome pleasure and a relief from the daily struggle. The *shtetl*, located in the midst of thick swamps and woods, was a place of hard-working craftsmen and merchants. A wooden synagogue occupied a prominent place in the village.

The rest of the population of Korzangorodok would have been indigenous people, Russians or Poles. These gentiles were landowners and peasants and neighbors who lived on the outskirts of town. Sometimes they were friendly, sometimes not.

The streets of the town may have been unpaved or, as it was in Yanova, paved in cobblestones. There would have been horses. Chickens, cats, and dogs roamed freely in the yards and across the roads. Market day was the liveliest day of the week, when people gathered in the town center to buy and sell poultry, produce, and other goods.

In the *shtetlach* there might be terrible poverty, where families with ten children lived in two-room shacks on bare earthen floors. Square, thatched-roof houses were commonplace among Jews in the *shtetl*. But, as in Yanova, there were also frame-and-brick houses and well-off Jewish families who had fewer children. As in most *shtetlach*, the fortunate ones, those who could be described as living with any degree of comfort, comprised only five percent of the population.

Many of the homes incorporated businesses. A clothing store might occupy one room in the front while the rest of the house was used for living quarters. Or a two-story house might feature a butcher shop or grocery on the first floor, while the family lived above the store. In Yanova and Rumshishok, the local forests provided lumber, and many Jews were involved in that trade. In Rumshishok, Jews owned a match factory as well as a sawmill.

Among the necessary ingredients required for a community to be classified as Jewish was, first and foremost, the synagogue. Then came the *mikveh* or ritual bath, and third was the *cheder*, a primary school for young children. These institutions gave form and structure to Jewish life. In an uncertain world constantly threatened by outside forces, people could look for guidance to the synagogue and the rabbi; the future was in the *cheder*, in the children who studied there, reading the Bible from morning into the evening hours.

Despite the fact that a Jew might live his entire life in a Korzangorodok or a Yanova and never leave, somehow he was still connected to other Jews throughout the Pale. For they, too, were going to *shul* and sending their children to *cheder* and preparing for the sabbath at sundown on Fridays. They may have lived separate lives in their own villages, but they had a shared existence.

It seems amazing that amid great difficulties and separation, a dispersed people struggled yet survived, their ancient religion, handed down from Abraham and Moses, sustaining them. Suffering misery and persecution, the Jews kept their covenant with God, studying and learning, for education was as much a part of their heritage as the Yiddish they spoke and the Talmud they revered. And through the years they maintained and passed on these traditions.

Grandpa Manson's town of Yanova was founded in 1775. The town developed because of its strategic position at the junction of the routes to the Baltic Sea and because it led to the St. Petersburg–Warsaw road. The industry of the area came from its forests—timber, carpentry, matches, and furniture.

In 1897 there were 3,975 Jews in Yanova, eighty percent of the town's population. In 1938 the Jewish population, which then numbered 3,000, was deported to Kovno (now known as Kaunas), where they were murdered by the Nazis.

Vilna, now known as Vilnuis, was the "Jerusalem of Lithuania." It was the commercial, intellectual, and cultural center for Jews in the Pale. In 1897 the Jewish population of the city was over 60,000, or forty-one percent of the total, and supported about one hundred synagogues. Today only one synagogue remains.

In a fascinating account of nineteenth-century Russian Jewish life, Chaim Aronson (1825–1888) writes in *A Jewish Life Under the Tsars* of being sent to "the vast city of Vilna" at age sixteen to study at the Yeshiva. He came from the Kovno district and went back in later years to teach there in the villages. My grandmother, Chana Aronzen or Aronson, also came from the Kovno district. I like to think that they may have been related.

Kovno itself was a large city. Its population was about 70,000, half of whom were Jewish. In 1887 the community supported twenty-five synagogues and prayer houses. Today the one remaining synagogue, a beautiful building, painted light blue and white, is attended by the present-day remnants of Kaunas Jews.

Whether they lived in the city or the *shtetl*, Jews who labored by hand had a hard life. A tailor might charge only twenty kopeks—ten cents—for making a shirt. There never was enough money, and some workers in the villages would occasionally receive produce or grain as partial payment for their efforts.

Besides merchants and craftsmen—carpenters like Grandpa Frumkin or cigar makers like Grandpa Manson—there were peddlers, harness makers, and bakers. There were also those who worked at trades that were exclusively Jewish. In addition to the rabbis and cantors and teachers, there were also the attendants in the *mikveh*, the matchmakers who arranged marriages, and "feather pluckers"—women who plucked freshly slaughtered kosher poultry so that the feathers could be used to stuff pillows.

Work was a fact of life in the *shtetl* but, apparently, not for everybody. The *shtetl* had its share of beggars, ne'er-do-wells, and what were called *luftmenshen*—those who seemed to live on air. This fanciful label suggests a certain tolerance and acceptance of those with little visible means of support. Describing his status, a so-called *luftmensch* said, "I'm a little bit of a *shammes*, a little bit a matchmaker. Before the holidays I sell palm branches for Sukkos; in the season I help out the tailor, and, besides, I have a brother in the United States who sends me every month a little something."*

The people of the *shtetl* were fairly tolerant—even protective—of aberrant behavior in their community. Perhaps they felt that with all the external threats to their existence, they had a responsibility to care for their own, to maintain the strength of their society, and that included its weakest links.

---

*Manners, Ande. *Poor Cousins*. pp. 32-33.

IV. What's in a Name?

What's in a name? That which we call a rose
By any other name would smell as sweet.

—Shakespeare

BOTH OF MY GRANDFATHERS underwent name changes. From Movschovitz or Manschowitz—or some other such variant—to Manson, and from Frumkin to Franklin. Almost every Jewish family has a similar tale to tell. For many American Jews, the original family name and the current name may share only a passing acquaintance with one another. From Movschovitz to Manson or Frumkin to Franklin is quite a sea change.

Crossing the ocean, an émigré carried a lot of baggage, including a name that was unfamiliar and perhaps difficult to pronounce. Immigration officials who greeted new arrivals at Castle Garden or Ellis Island might impatiently write down what was easier rather than what was accurate. Therefore, Sadlowdky became Sadler or Abromsky became Abel. But sometimes the oft-maligned immigration official was not the culprit.

Justin Kaplan and Anne Bernays, in their 1997 book, *The Language of Names*, quote historian Robert Rennick, who maintains that names written on the ship's manifest were often misspelled or otherwise mutilated, a consequence of harried and hurried ship's officials confronting unlettered and confused emigrants amid the chaos of embarking on an ocean voyage.

My husband tells a story he heard many years ago from a college friend whose grandfather made the journey to America, as did many others, alone and with very little money. Aboard the ship he struck up a friendship with another emigrant, and throughout the long passage they shared their hopes and dreams, spinning tales of what life would be like in America and perhaps trying to ease the pain of leaving behind all they had known.

When they reached the port of Boston, each planning to depart for different destinations, knowing that in all likelihood they would never see each other again, they wanted to exchange something, a memento, something to remember each other by. But what? They were poor; they had nothing, nothing to give. Except for one thing: their names. So one man got Alpert and the other man got an unpronounceable string of syllables.

But one of the best tales—and it is just that, a tale—illustrates just how prevalent was the practice of getting an instant name change upon arriving in the new country. Every Jewish family will tell you about the Jew named Shane Ferguson. They will speak of him as if they knew him, as if he were a distant cousin. "Oh you don't know about Shane Ferguson?" they would ask gleefully. "Oh, sure, he arrived at Ellis Island, and when the immigration officer asked him his name, so eager to be a new American, he just says 'Shoyn fergessen.' That's Yiddish for 'I've already forgotten.'"

But whether name changes were voluntary or involuntary for the Jewish immigrant family, the fact is that they happened quite regularly. And not always instantly. My mother's father changed his name more than twenty years after arriving in America. In 1910, when Grandpa got a new name, his petition to city hall for a name change states that since his son Charles had already changed his name to Franklin, "it made it less confusing for delivery of mail." And that was how Wolf Frumkin became William Franklin.

There was another reason for changing an obviously Jewish-sounding name: anti-Semitism. A name that sounded Jewish could provoke certain unpleasantries. At the very least, you might have a name that people laughed at. At worst, your name might invite antipathy and hostility.

Americanized names were easier, no question about it. No more being asked "How do you spell that?" No more mispronunciations. And people were less likely to embarrass you or make fun of you if your name was Manson rather than Movschovitz. (Of course, this was all decades before the infamous murderer Charles Manson came on the scene, imparting a terrible odor to the name. One hopes it is a temporary fall from grace for this good and worthy name.)

"A self-made man may prefer a self-made name." That's what Judge Learned Hand said when Sam Gelbfisch changed his name to Samuel Goldwyn. Anyway, how would it have looked on the silver screen—Metro, Gelbfisch, and Mayer?

Sam Goldwyn, who had come out of Russia with very little but the clothes on his back, worked as a peddler when he first came to this country. He helped establish the fledgling movie industry and became one of its giants.

In years past, more so than now, if you were in the movie business you changed your name. Particularly if you were an actress or an actor and the studio executives told you your name had to look good on the marquee or up there on the screen. Or sound good on the radio.

Nathan Birnbaum became George Burns. Benny Kubelsky became Jack Benny. Fanny Borach became Fanny Brice. Bernie Schwartz became Tony Curtis. The great star of Broadway musicals, Ethel Merman got her name when she lopped off the Zim from Zimmerman. It got so that if you heard that one of your favorite stars of the silver screen was Jewish, you automatically responded, "Oh, yeah? What was her real name?"

Maybe it just made us feel that if someone name Goldberg or Cohen or Schwartz could become a movie star, well, maybe achieving such glory wasn't totally impossible. Maybe your cousin Elliot really would be an actor; maybe you would, or I....

Today, of course, it is more acceptable to have an ethnic name or aspect. Who knows? Maybe things have turned around so much that acquiring a Jewish name could be a step toward success. And where did Whoopi Goldberg get that moniker, anyway?

Perhaps it started with Barbra Streisand, who didn't change her name—or her nose. And proving that you don't have to be Jewish to succeed, there's Al Pacino and Robert De Niro. Today's social and political atmosphere is more realistic in acknowledging the diversity and multicultural makeup of our society, rather than denying them. Anyway, we might all agree that it looks better to have an image of a more substantial, genuine person. Nobody wants to appear artificial or shallow—even if they are.

The name game is endlessly fascinating. The connections can be surprising. For example, when reading about life in the old country, I will occasionally come upon names that resonate with familiarity. A relative, I wonder? Could it be? Who is Bernard Maneshewitz, described as "one of Kovno's leading well-to-do Jews" in Lucy Dawidowicz's *The Golden Tradition*? My father's people came from the Vilna/Kovno district, and the name Movschovitz was easily subject to various spellings. Of course, I must admit I never heard any references in our family to ancestors who were "well-to-do." But you never know.

Or what about the story that we are related to a bullfighter? Some family members on my mother's side seem to put some credence in this one, and though I love the story and would like to believe it, I have my doubts as to its authenticity.

The origin of this tale lies in the fact that there really was an American bullfighter, Sidney Franklin. Born in Brooklyn, he achieved a good deal of renown, making his debut in Spain in 1929. He became a friend of the great Ernest Hemingway, who described Franklin in *Death in the Afternoon* as "one of the most skillful, graceful, and slow manipulators of the cape in his day." Franklin's original name was Frumkin.

Besides a matador, our family tree may also hold musicians. An early piece of sheet music dating from 1910 and published by the Hebrew Publishing Company in New York lists a Yiddish song with "words by M. Aronson [and] music composed and arranged by J.M. Rumshisky." There has to be a connection there, I am sure. My grandmother's maiden name was Aronson. The surname Rumshisky most certainly comes from Rumsiskes, where my grandfather Manson was married.

Among immigrants, there is ample precedent for assuming the name of one's birthplace as one's own. It happened in fact, and it happened in fiction. We need only look at Mario Puzo's *The Godfather* to see how Vito Andolini, upon leaving his home in Italy, became Vito Corleone in the New World, taking his new family name from his old town of Corleone.

There was a time when family names didn't exist. Before 1800, the majority of Jews in Europe had no surnames. A person might have been identified by his trade, as in "Wolf the Carpenter." And if there was another carpenter in town named Wolf? Then perhaps he would be known by his father's name, as in "Wolf the son of Hillel." Or there might be Wolf the Carpenter and Wolf the Shoemaker. Other identifications might have been made by citing the town a person came from: "Zelda from Korzangorodok."

In 1804, an edict came down from the czar requiring Jews to adopt surnames. This was done in order to facilitate a census count. The sources for the new names came from common references—geography, for one. Thus names such as Berliner, Moscowitz, and, as we have seen, Rumshisky came into being, names that identified the cities and towns the people came from.

A person's occupation was also a way to establish a new name. The Yiddish name for baker was Becker, a tailor was a Schneider, and a leather worker was a Lederer.

One family chose its name because the order to select a surname was received on a holiday, when there were sweets and almonds out on the table. The Yiddish name for almonds is *mandlen*, and the family adopted the name Mandelkern. They probably also had flowers on the table; had

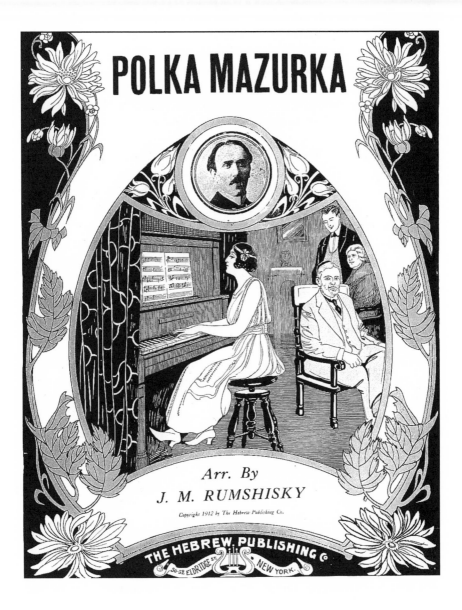

POLKA MAZURKA

Arr. By

J. M. RUMSHISKY

Copyright 1912 by The Hebrew Publishing Co.

THE HEBREW PUBLISHING Co.
50-52 ELDRIDGE St.   NEW YORK

I been a member of that family I might have urged the adoption of Blum instead of Mandelkern. Or undoubtedly they had a white tablecloth; Weiss would be nice. The possibilities are intriguing.

Other names were connected to stones and flowers: Silver, Gold, Diamond, Bloom, Rosen. And Rothstein, which means red stone. It was almost two hundred years ago that these names, family names, were established.

Yet another way that surnames were chosen hearkens back to a time when street addresses did not exist in the towns of Europe, and families hung wooden signs with symbols or pictures on them over their doors. Thus a picture of a cat would lead to the family name Katz.

Although some of the ways in which people adopted names are surely amusing, the reasons necessitating such actions are far less so. The persecution that Jews suffered, the denial of liberty and rights, were conditions that contributed to the loss—or lack—of a name. And Jews, of course, were not the only ones who suffered. Black Americans, brought to this country as slaves, lost everything they had, including their names, in Africa. The surnames they acquired were those of the slave masters.

For Jews arriving in America, changing one's name was a common occurrence. There is a story about the fellow who runs into an old acquaintance and says:

"Shmuel Rabinowitz! Haven't seen you for years!"

"Shah," says Shmuel, "that's not my name anymore. Too old-country. Now I'm C.D. Rivington."

"How'd you think of that?"

"You know, I used to *shlep* fruit on Rivington Street."

"Then what's the C.D.?"

"Corner Delancey."*

In the popular 1980s movie *Splash*, the beautiful mermaid played by Daryll Hanna likes the sound of the name Madison, picked from a street sign on the upper East Side of Manhattan. Culturally, Madison Avenue is a long way from Rivington Street, but it would seem that human nature hasn't changed much through the years: if the name fits, wear it.

---

*Shepard and Levi. *Live and Be Well.* p. 121.

V. Pogrom

Nisht alleh tsores kumen fun himmel.
(Not all troubles come from heaven.)

—*Yiddish proverb*

ON MAY 19, 1903, A RALLY was held in Boston's Faneuil Hall, a hallowed place of citizen protests since revolutionary days. Very likely the Movschovitz family with five-year-old Frankie—my father—and the Frumkin family with three-year-old Fannie—my mother—were there. So many Jews were. They were there, as in other cities around the world, to demonstrate their anguish over the Kishinev Massacre.

During Passover, at noon on Sunday, the town of Kishinev became the scene of death and destruction. Russian troops stood by while a mob of rioters attacked the Jewish quarter. Wielding axes and clubs, they murdered forty-nine Jews. Hundreds were injured, thousands left homeless, and 1,500 homes and shops were looted and destroyed.

The Boston Globe of May 28 that year added its somewhat muted voice to the outcry against the brutal Kishinev pogrom. Nothing, it said, could prevent "human beings in one part of the world from sincerely sympathizing with…men, women and children in another country, and letting them who are responsible for misery know that their acts are deplored and censured."

Pogrom (Russian) means an attack on Jews by a mob of Christians. Yet that sanitized definition does not begin to impart the terror that the word conjured up in the hearts and minds of *shtetl* Jews. They lived with the fear that perhaps late at night, after too much drinking or upon the capricious whim of the head of the local police, the Cossacks might ride into a Jewish village, destroying, looting, setting fire to homes, killing.

43

But why? Why did such things happen? Why, for that matter, does anti-Semitism exist? How can we understand a policy of hatred based on race or religion?

"Everything that is rotten in the world," said the anti-Semite to the Jew, "is the fault of the Jews."

"That's true," said the Jew with great conviction. "You're absolutely right. The Jews and the people who eat bananas."

"Why people who eat bananas?"

"Why Jews?"*

Why indeed? From what we know of prejudice and tyranny, they are perpetuated against those who are perceived as different, separate from the majority. The tyrant can take the form of a czar, a Hitler, or a school-yard bully. The need to build oneself up by victimizing someone else is an aspect of the mentality of hatred.

Jews, with their own history, language, religious practices, and culture—even their own laws, dietary and otherwise—were prime targets of suspicion. Living apart and separate, a condition which, ironically, was forced upon them, made the Jew "different." It is all too easy to attribute base or malevolent behavior to those whom we perceive to be different.

The Russian or Polish peasant, poor though he was, knew that there was someone lower than he on the social ladder: the Jew. He also knew that malicious acts against the Jew would not only be tolerated by the government, the czar and the police; they would be encouraged. For this was a government that could condone the pogroms by asserting that Jews were socialists, a dreadful and untrustworthy thing to be.

But as history tells us, it is never difficult to rationalize racial and religious hatred, especially when poverty and repression exist. These were conditions affecting Christians as well as Jews. Illiterate peasants, looking for their meager crust of bread, often regarded Jews as rivals for the few jobs available. And the government knew that the discontent of the peasantry, instead of being directed toward them, might be alleviated by a night's rioting in the Jewish quarter or in the *shtetl*. Nothing like swooping down on a village, burning and destroying Jewish homes, to take your mind off your own troubles.

It happened in Korzangorodok, in Yanova, and in Rumshishok. Records show that in 1915 there were armed attacks by Cossacks in Rumshishok. The town memorial book (Yizkor) tells of people gathering up their belongings to flee the town in their wagons. If they had no horse or buggy, they left on foot.

---

*Van Den Haag, Ernest. *The Jewish Mystique*. p. 65.

Persecution, exile and exodus: words that evoke terror and awe, they have too often been the fate of the Jew. Since biblical days, from the time of Moses, when the first exodus of the Jews took place, an anguished tale has unfolded of a people seeking freedom.

"Now, therefore, behold, the cry of the children of Israel is come unto me: and I have also seen the oppression wherewith the Egyptians oppress them. And now then go, and I will send thee unto Pharaoh, and thou shalt bring forth my people the children of Israel out of Egypt," Exodus 3:9–11.

"Let my people go," was the cry of Moses to the Pharaoh, a cry that has echoed through the ages to other despots such as the hated Torquemada, who, in fifteenth-century Spain, ushered in a reign of terror.

King Ferdinand and Queen Isabella may live in American history as the patrons of Columbus, the sponsors of his epic 1492 journey to the New World; but they are also remembered as being influenced by Torquemada, whose evil genius guided the Inquisition. In that historic year of 1492—a year that would bring glory and riches to Spain—Ferdinand and Isabella signed an edict directed at all Jews in Spain: Jews must convert to Catholicism; failure to do so would result in being burned at the stake.

In modern times, in this enlightened twentieth century, "let my people go" rang out again as one of the most cataclysmic events in human history occurred. The Third Reich was established in Nazi Germany under its leader, Adolf Hitler. It was Hitler who presided over the Holocaust, the systematic murder of European Jewry, which took 6 million Jewish lives. It is a number and an event impossible to comprehend, but even more impossible to forget.

There was no Moses to lead the Jews out of Spain in 1492 or out of Germany in 1942. And in nineteenth-century Russia, with the exception of Alexander II's reign from 1855 to 1881, a time of comparative peace, Jewish existence under the czar was marginal at best: fragile, insecure, and difficult. At worst, there was persecution and death.

Pogroms had taken place in Russia before, notably in Odessa in 1817. But after 1881, after Alexander II's assassination, they increased. Almost immediately, anti-Jewish riots began. In the district of Kiev there were pogroms in forty-eight towns, and they spread rapidly to other districts. Thousands of Jews were left homeless.

The new czar, Alexander III, didn't need any encouragement in carrying out government-sponsored strikes against Jews. But he certainly was abetted by some of his advisors, who were virulently anti-Semitic. Of them, Alexander's former tutor Pobedonostsov was most influential.

Pobedonostsov was opposed to any democratic spirit in Russia and obsessively committed to the ideal of "Mother Russia" in much the same way as Hitler would be to the notion of Aryan purity in the German Fatherland. He is credited with devising the sinister plan to purge Russia of its Jews. The plan was based on disposing of the Jewish population by thirds. By establishing a regime of brutality, one-third of the Jews would die, one-third would emigrate, and one-third would be absorbed into Russian culture. This was the rationale, the *raison d'etre*, for the cruel May Laws of 1882, laws which effectually established a permanent pogrom.

The noted Yiddish writer Sholom Aleichem penned a letter in 1905 that is a vivid description of a pogrom and a plea for world attention.

> ...A rumor was spread abroad that orders had been given to attack the Jews—and the attack began from all sides. Simultaneously, an order was issued that we should not shoot from the windows, and not throw stones. If we should do that, the soldiers would fire back and destroy our houses. Seeing soldiers on the street—and Cossacks—we felt reassured; and they did help, but not us...
>
> They helped to rob, to beat, to ravish, to despoil. Before our eyes and in the eyes of the whole world, they helped to smash windows, break down doors, break locks and to put booty in their pockets. Before our eyes and in the eyes of our children, they beat Jews grievously—men, women, and children—and they shouted, "Money, give us your money." Before our eyes women were hurled from windows and children thrown to the cobblestones...

The work of Sholom Aleichem, himself an émigré to America, gave testimony to the struggles of the *shtetl* Jew. It is the *shtetl* Jew who turned increasingly away from Russia, knowing that life in that country was a cursed existence with limited resources and even less hope.

For many—particularly those who believed in Zionism and the establishment of a Jewish homeland—Palestine, the land of the Bible, the land of milk and honey, held out hope for a better future. For many more, that hope was in America. Jews at Passover began substituting the traditional prayer of "next year in Jerusalem" with "next year in America."

As Chaim Aronson wrote in *A Jewish Life Under the Tsars*, "During 1882, I received letters form New York—from my wife's brother...who had fled from the rioters when they had attacked the Jewish districts of

Kiev.... He was followed by his brother Saul.... They took their wives and sons and daughters and found a good living in the new land."

With time, the number of Russian Jews seeking a way out to freedom grew. In 1870, about 1,000 Jews came to America. By 1882, that number had grown to 21,000. And in 1889, the year my Grandfather Franklin crossed the ocean by himself, he was one of 81,000 Russian Jews seeking a new life in the New World.*

---

*Schoener, Allon, ed. *Portal to America.* p. 24.

VI: Leaving the Old World

*Democracy is always a beckoning goal, not a safe harbor.
For freedom is an unremitting endeavor, never a final
achievement.*

—*Supreme Court Justice Felix Frankfurter*

"THE DAY I LEFT HOME, my mother came with me to the railroad station. When we said goodbye, she said it was just like seeing me go into my casket. I never saw her again."*

Those wrenching words come from a Jewish immigrant from Lithuania, but they most certainly could have been echoed by any number of Russian Jews. When Harris and Annie Movschovitz left Lithuania in 1892, they too left behind parents and relatives never to be seen again.

In 1911, the Boston City Directory listed a Joseph Manschowitz (sic) living at the same address with a Harris. Was he a younger brother newly arrived in America? I had never heard of an Uncle Joe. Perhaps he was not a brother, but a cousin. The connections and the losses are a source of speculation, questions upon questions, some never to be answered.

But even with family separation and fear of the unknown, even with anxieties about the New World, the hope held out by America was irresistible. And yet, even before they could think of what awaited them there across the ocean, Russia's Jews would encounter enormous difficulties in their attempts to leave the Old World.

They may have left their villages on foot, with bundles and carts carrying all their worldly possessions. Or they may have had enough mon-

---

*Chermayeff, Ivan; Wasserman, Fred and Shapiro, Mary. *Ellis Island.*

ey for a third-class railway ticket, which would get them to the border. Then perhaps a little more money was needed to bribe border officials so they could cross into Germany where boats from one of the northern ports such as Bremen or Hamburg would be sailing to America. And, of course, still more money was needed for passage on one of the great ocean liners.

To the many immigrants who had never been much beyond their villages, the noise and confusion of the cities brought anxiety. And excitement. For most, it would be the first time they had seen electric lights. Something as simple and commonplace as a banana was a new and novel experience.

Then as now, papers and passports were required for travel in Europe. But for Jews, who were less than full citizens, unable to own property, abused and restricted in so many ways, the simple matter of a passport was not so simple.

In czarist Russia, passports were denied these would-be émigrés. And if somehow one was able to secure a passport, the requirements could be fairly daunting as well as costly. About half a dozen permits and travel documents were needed; one might have to journey to a city where government officials would issue these all-important papers. The process could take months, even years. Needless to say, many people chose to bypass this procedure for one more expedient, but one not without danger.

"It was two o'clock in the morning when my guide, whose business it was to smuggle travelers without passports to Germany, called for me.... After walking silently in the dark for about an hour, we reached a forest near the frontier, about three miles north of the regular gate. From behind trees we could see and hear the guards marching to and fro. In a few moments we heard the shots of revolvers from a distance; this usually meant that contraband runners were being fired upon. 'Let us go now!' said my guide. 'The soldiers are now busy with the contraband runner, and we can safely pass the boundary line.' I crossed the boundary line without the slightest mishap...."*

Dramatic as this description of one Jewish immigrant's experience may be, illegal border crossings were commonplace. There were four major routes out of Russia: from the Austro-Hungarian Empire one crossed into Germany, on to Berlin and the north. From Romania the trek led through Vienna, Frankfurt, and Amsterdam. From southern Russia and the Ukraine, the route took émigrés across the Austro-Hun-

---

*Karp, Abraham. *The Golden Door to America.* p. 71.

garian border and then northward. For the vast majority of émigrés, those coming from Lithuania or from Minsk—people like my grandparents—illegal crossings into Germany were the only way out.

Crossing borders meant dealing with border patrols. The soldiers who guarded the borders were eager to supplement their meager incomes with bribes. Desperate to get out of Russia, the émigrés knew that they must be prepared to offer them money, money they could scarcely spare but which was more affordable than the costly passports and certificates demanded by the government bureaucracy. Many Russian officials, it was said, did a thriving business smuggling Jews across the border.

Money was always an issue for the poor Jews of Russia. Whereas before they had worried about how to get enough to live, now they worried about how to get enough to leave. Crossing the Atlantic in steerage might cost as little as fifteen dollars or as much as thirty-five dollars. At the turn of the century an average worker's salary might be five dollars a week, so the sum of thirty-five dollars was not inconsiderable.

We have all heard about the voyage across the Atlantic and how our ancestors traveled in steerage and suffered miserably during the crossing. Steerage was the underbelly of the ship where the steering mechanisms were located. Perhaps as many as 2,000 people were packed into the damp, dirty quarters, men and women in separate quarters, sleeping in three layers of bunk beds with straw or seaweed-stuffed mattresses. These émigré passengers were jammed in like so much freight, while above-decks wealthy travelers enjoyed the pleasures of a luxurious ocean voyage.

While it usually took ten to seventeen days to cross the ocean, many émigrés were put on older, slower ships on which the journey could take as much as three weeks. The great "greyhounds of the sea," as the ocean liners were called, loaded their human cargo, carrying them in conditions that were nothing less than appalling. The food was terrible; there was little air or ventilation. Seasickness was rampant.

"The vomitings of the seasick are often permitted to remain a long time before being removed. The floors, when iron, are continually damp, and when of wood they reek with foul odor because they are not washed."*

"Everyone had smelly food, and the atmosphere was so thick and dense with smoke and bodily odors that your head itched, and when you went to scratch your head you got lice in your hands. We had six weeks of that."†

*Manners, Ande. *Poor Cousins.* p 55
†Chermayeff, Ivan, et al. *Ellis Island.*

Many of the passengers were Jews who would eat nothing but kosher food; for them the journey was even more difficult. They ate nothing but the bread and herring they brought with them, sometimes asking only for hot water into which they would put a little sugar or brandy for flavor.

In addition to the real hardships experienced, there were those created by imagination and anxiety. For people who had known provincial village life, new and overwhelming events occurred almost daily. They had fled across borders, perhaps been smuggled across at midnight. They had journeyed on foot or by train to seaports where they were crammed into the bellies of huge ships setting out across a vast ocean. They were poor, they were hungry, and they were unsure of what was happening to them, unsure of what *would* happen to them, what awaited them in this new place called America.

There were irrational fears and there were realistic ones. For people of limited experience who, in all likelihood, had never set foot off the land, the idea of traveling on water, often rough water, was frightening. Perhaps these giant ships, these behemoths, would collide! A ship could sink, and instead of the New World what really awaited one would be a watery grave. In some instances this was not just a fear but a reality. One immigrant account tells of a fifteen-day crossing during which thirty-two people died of cholera and were buried at sea.*

In addition to all the real and imagined terrors suffered by the Jew, there was also the anxiety of the very religious about how to *be* a Jew in America. Everyone had heard tales of countrymen who had gone to America, shaved off their beards, put aside their old ways, and adopted the customs of the new country. They didn't even keep kosher anymore; was that possible? If you didn't keep the sabbath by being a pious, observant Jew, if you didn't keep a kosher home but instead ate God-knows-what kind of "treyf" food, then what kind of Jew were you? If you lost your Jewishness, which was the very soul of your being, then what were you gaining?

But despite the fears, they came. They came by the hundreds and by the thousands. While it is true that two thirds of Eastern European Jews remained where they were, between 1880 and 1914 more than two million of the five million Jews living in Eastern Europe emigrated to America. Four of them were my grandparents.

These émigrés, traveling with burdens and fears, carried with them other travel companions. There was hope and there was a dauntless will not only to survive, but to thrive. Improbable though it may seem, there

---

*Schoener, Allon, *The American Jewish Album*. p. 112.

"The Steerage" by Alfred Stieglitz
COURTESY OF THE MUSEUM OF THE CITY OF NEW YORK

were even laughter and gaiety. Mary Antin, who left her home in Polotsk, Russia, in 1894 with her mother and sisters to join her father in America, describes her voyage in *The Promised Land*. She talks of the "torments of seasickness" and the "perils of the sea," but there were also "happy hours on deck, with fugitive sunshine, birds atop the crested waves, band music and dancing and fun. I explored the ship, made friends with officers and crew, or pursued my thoughts in quiet nooks. It was my first experience of the ocean, and I was profoundly moved."

After seventeen days at sea, the boat carrying her and her family arrived at the port of Boston. "The morning was glorious.... The sky was clear and blue, the sun shone brightly.... And soon, oh joyful sight!, we saw the tops of two trees! What a shout there rose! Everyone pointed out the welcome sight to everybody else, as if they did not see it.... Then steamers and boats of all kinds passed by, in all directions.... Oh, what a beautiful scene! No corner of the earth is half so fair as the lovely picture before us...."

Mary Antin's accounts of her "marvelous adventures of...American life," which appear in her two other books, are nothing less than thrilling. This brilliant girl, who took to learning and books the way a duck does to water, who went on to Boston Latin School and then Barnard College, never got over the wonder of her new life. "That I who was born in the prison of the Pale should roam at will in the land of freedom was a marvel that it did me good to realize." In keeping with Jewish tradition, she held to the biblical exhortation we are all impelled to obey, one that we intone each year at Passover: "Remember the days of thy going forth out of the land of Egypt all the days of thy life."

VII. The Goldene Medina

So at last I was going to America! Really, really going at last! The boundaries burst. The arch of heaven soared. A million suns shone out for every star. The winds rushed in from outer space, roaring in my ears, "America! America!

—Mary Antin, The Promised Land

AFTER ALL THE HARDSHIPS of life in Russia, after the struggle to leave that life behind, after the great difficulties endured in arranging the journey to the New World, at last they were "off for America. Where it is, I don't know. I only know it's far. You have to ride and ride until you get there. And when you get there, there's a Kestel Gartel where they undress you and look you in the eyes."

Kestel Gartel, in the inimitable immigrant dialect of the great storyteller Sholom Aleichem, was Castle Garden, the citadel of freedom, the processing center in New York through which some eight million immigrants entered America in the years 1855 to 1890. From January 1, 1892, until 1947, Ellis Island in New York harbor was the station through which twenty million people came into the United States. For two years prior to that, the Barge Office at the Battery had been used for immigration.

But, whether it was "Kestel Gartel" or Ellis Island or an immigration office in East Boston, the immigration center was perceived by new arrivals as one more obstacle on their long road to freedom. These were centers where masses of people were herded together, subjected to rigorous physical examinations, and put through question-and-answer sessions in a language most did not understand. At their worst, immigration centers were fearful places where people could be detained or, in the case of illness, quarantined or, even returned to the countries of their origin.

"...All I remember of Ellis Island," recalled one woman, "was a very, very sad place. People were deathly afraid that they might be diseased or hard of hearing or something, because right away, oh, before we even got onto Ellis, we were deloused. I can even smell it. Like kerosene in the hair. It was a very unattractive place. People just huddled together; families huddled together and they were all afraid lest they be sent back or not allowed...."*

This was the glory of America? For the Russian Jews who had lived under the terrible reign of the Cossacks, it was frightening to encounter still more uniformed officials, officials who could be brusque, impatient, and thoroughly intimidating. To some it felt like Judgment Day when they had to prove themselves worthy to enter the "golden land."

The very uniforms of an official frightened many of the immigrants. That was one of the things from which they were escaping; now one of the first sights they encountered was that of a uniformed official, something they thought had been left behind with other bad memories on the other side of the ocean.

At Ellis Island, the main building had a great room on one floor where baggage was taken. There was another great room on the upper floor where the immigrants were sent. Every immigrant wore a tag with a number. Immigration officers might deal with as many as 5,000 people a day. There were lines; there was confusion; there was waiting. It was not uncommon for belongings to be lost or displaced, perhaps never to be found.

The actual inspection of each person usually took less than forty-five minutes. "What's your name? Where are you going? What is your trade? How much money do you have?" Interpreters and officials queried the newly arrived immigrant, alarming him with questions ranging from his family background to his political views. People were unsure as to how to respond. "If I say I have no money, will they still let me in? What should I answer?" The apprehensions of the new arrivals were, for the most part, unfounded. The answers to the questions might be of less importance than the ability to answer at all, since the officials were also on the lookout for those who were deaf or dumb.

The medical examinations to which each immigrant was subjected really were cause for alarm. The initial exam took only minutes as the doctors checked for tuberculosis, mental disorders, and trachoma, a highly contagious eye disease which, if left untreated, could cause blindness.

---

*Simons, Howard. *Jewish Times.* p. 37.

The scalp and throat were examined as doctors looked for signs of infection. The vast majority of those inspected were approved for entry and given a card marked "Admitted." Those who did not pass the medical exams had their clothing marked with a piece of chalk—L for lameness, Ct for trachoma, H for heart, and so on. Those so labeled were detained for further examination.

Twenty percent of the immigrants were thus detained. They might be quarantined for a while, treated, and then released. Only two percent were deported. While the percentage was low, to those who suffered the fate of deportation it was the cruelest blow in a long series of bitter struggles. To be forced to return to a country from which one had fled for one's life was more than some could take. Through its forty years of immigrant activity, Ellis Island was the scene of 3,000 suicides. Small wonder that the place had the unhappy sobriquet of "Island of Tears," the tears of those not allowed to set foot on American soil.

If my grandparents arrived at the port of New York, as seventy percent of all immigrants did, Wolf Frumkin would have been processed through Castle Garden in 1889 or 1890. Built in 1807 as Fort Clinton, it enjoyed a brief period as a concert hall, and the famed soprano Jenny Lind sang there in 1850. Later, from 1900 to 1941, it was the New York Aquarium, and today it serves as a ticket office for those purchasing tickets for the trip to Ellis Island.

Arriving in 1892 Harris and Annie Movschovitz would have come through Ellis Island. More than half of the Jews headed for Boston entered America through the port of New York. Surely they would have been on deck with the other passengers, awed by the sight of their first American city. But one other sight would have dazzled them, as it has every new arrival to these shores since 1886. That was the year when the Statue of Liberty arrived in New York, a gift of the French in commemoration of the French and American revolutions. "Lady Liberty," raising her torch of freedom to the sky, stands 156 feet high and is perhaps the most recognized symbol of liberty the world over.

Boston, where my grandparents settled, was the second-busiest port in America. Though it could claim no magnificent statue in its harbor, Boston would have aroused the same emotions in the hearts of new arrivals as did New York. If Grandpa and Grandma Movschovitz came to Boston directly, they would have docked at the East Boston Immigration Building, where they would have undergone an entry procedure similar to that experienced by those at Castle Garden or Ellis Island.

Wolf Frumkin was the first of his family to arrive in America. His brother Morris, older by two years, did not come until 1910, and as a child I remember visiting with one of his daughters, my mother's cousin Mary Mogul. Abraham Mendel, the third brother, never emigrated to America, but his youngest son, Israel, did, establishing a home in Ohio, where some of his descendants still live.

When Wolf Frumkin arrived in America in 1889 he was thirty-one years old and alone. When he said goodbye to his wife and three little children, he did not know how long it would be before he would see them again. He had very little money, but he was prepared to work hard at his trade of carpenter/builder in order to save as much as he could as quickly as he could. It would take him five years to save enough so that his family could finally join him.

More than likely, he was similar to most of the Jewish immigrants pouring into America. For one thing, he was not very religious. The most pious Jews were not so interested in coming to a country where Jews shaved their beards and women discarded their wigs. Surely, they thought, it was a heathen nation where their *Yiddishkeit*, their Jewish way of life, could not thrive.

Besides being non-religious, Wolf, like most of his fellow Jewish immigrants, was poor. Half of the newly arrived immigrants had no money at all; the average amount they entered with was around fifteen dollars. Many were artisans and laborers. Fully half of them were in the needle trades. The rest were butchers, bakers, clerks, and merchants. In addition to being poor, the masses of Jewish immigrants were also uneducated. However, there was a core of Jewish intellectuals, writers, journalists, and poets who, seeking personal freedom, fled to America, a place where they could write and speak out without fear of reprisals from the government.

When the first heavy waves of immigration began in America, there were only about 250,000 Jews in the country. These people, earlier arrivals, many of whom had come from Germany around 1848, were neither uneducated nor poor. Some of them, in fact, were quite wealthy. Needless to say, they had mixed feelings about welcoming fellow Jews who had little in common with them except their religious heritage.

Among those Jewish families well established in America was that of Emma Lazarus, the author of *The New Colossus*. (Unfortunately, she died before she knew that her words would be immortalized on the base of the Statue of Liberty and in the hearts and minds of millions as a ringing testimony to freedom.) How ironic that this woman, who penned those inspirational words welcoming the "wretched refuse" of other lands, was herself from a wealthy, assimilated Sephardic Jewish family. The Lazarus family enjoyed a very comfortable life in America, one quite remote from that of the hordes of Eastern European Jews washing up on

America's shores in the late nineteenth century. Indeed, the gulf between the Lazarus family and their coreligionists was enormous; Emma's sister Anna once referred to one of Emma's acquaintances as "one of my sister's Jewish friends."

The new arrivals, "the huddled masses," must have seemed uncivilized—and worse—to Jews of such prominence as the Lazarus family and the other great New York Jewish families, people with names like Straus and Schiff, Goldman and Sachs, Loeb and Guggenheim and Lehman. These were people who had established the great commercial and banking institutions of New York, people who lived in the grand mansions that lined Fifth Avenue, who had French chefs and English butlers and who gave teas and coming-out parties.

These were people who were enormously wealthy and who created some of the most successful business enterprises in the world—department stores such as Macy's and Gimbel's, banking and investment businesses like Kuhn, Loeb & Co., or Goldman Sachs. They built New York's renowned Jewish Reform synagogue, Temple Emanu-El. And they would produce a New York governor and later United States Senator, Herbert Lehman, as well as such gifts for New York and the world as the Guggenheim Museum.

Little wonder that the new Jewish immigrants from Eastern Europe appeared to these grandees as aliens. Dressed in peasant clothes, the immigrant women wore kerchiefs or *babushkas* on their heads. The men wore the long caftans and full beards that marked the orthodox Jew. The new arrivals carried all their worldly goods with them—clothes, family pictures, linens, personal treasures. The brass candlesticks that today stand on the breakfront in my dining room were brought over by my Grandmother Jennie Frumkin when she came to join Wolf in 1894.

The "Germans"—as the uptown wealthy established Jews were called—developed philanthropic means to help the downtrodden—and downtown—"Russians," the all-inclusive name for the new Jewish immigrants. (Whether they came from the Ukraine, Romania, Poland or Lithuania, did not matter; they were the "Russians.") The Germans thought of themselves as Americans. They were nothing like these other Jews, these Russians, poor and speaking the vulgar language of Yiddish. And there were so many of them. By 1918 there would be over 2,500,000 Russian Jews in America, ten times the number of German Jews.

The Germans were distressed about the hordes of Russians—the great unwashed—descending upon them. As one Boston (German) Rabbi put it, the Russians were "a bane to the country and a curse to the

Jews." As a statement from a man of God, this sentiment seems peculiarly lacking in charity and brotherly love. But fortunately there were others who exhibited a more generous spirit. At the 1892 dedication of Boston's Hebrew Sheltering Home, Abraham Spitz said, "We...can hardly realize the persecutions to which our coreligionists in Russia have been subjected.... We must and shall receive them with open arms.... We must teach them the manners and customs of an enlightened community...thus enabling them to become useful and desirable citizens."*

Despite the economic and emotional gulf that separated the Germans and the Russians, despite the baser feelings expressed by some, there was no denying their common heritage. They all were Jewish.

Charities were established to assist the new immigrants. The United Hebrew Charities provided room and board and medical care as well as lectures and information that would advise the Russians and educate them to the ways of America. As Stephen Birmingham points out in *Our Crowd*, "Money was given largely but grudgingly...out of a hard, bitter sense of resentment, embarrassment, and worry over what the neighbors would think...." The Germans, however reluctantly, gave millions to aid the Russians in the form of food, shelter, travel assistance, and jobs.

One of the most successful aid organizations was HIAS, the Hebrew Immigrant Aid Society, established in 1892. It grew out of a self-help group of Eastern Europeans, not of Germans. Newly arrived immigrants at Ellis Island could be certain that a HIAS representative would be there to interpret, advise, and in general to facilitate matters for them.

HIAS helped immigrants get settled, perhaps placing them with relatives, and assisted in finding employment for them. As advocates for the immigrant Jew, they offered countless thousands shelter, education, and legal assistance. They could answer such basic questions as which street car one should take to get to one's destination. Upon arrival at Ellis Island, the Russian Jews knew they could look for help from the people wearing blue caps with the Yiddish letters HIAS stitched on them. Sometimes, despite the assistance, confusion still existed. The story is told—and perhaps it is just a story—of the newly arrived immigrant, just off the boat, who is standing on a street corner, counting the streetcars as they rumble by. When asked why he is doing this, he replies, "Well, I was told to take streetcar number fifty-two and so far, only fourteen streetcars have gone by."

In addition to traditional aid societies, there was the power of the

---

*Sarna, Jonathan D. and Smith, Ellen. *The Jews of Boston.* p. 242.

press to aid the newcomers. Many newspapers published stories about
the deplorable condition of the immigrants. Among these influential papers was the major Yiddish-language daily in America, the *Jewish Daily
Forward.* It was founded in 1897 by Abraham Cahan, himself an immigrant from Lithuania, who edited it until his death in 1951. The paper
generated articles and protests and caught the attention of Americans,
including official America. In 1909 the government launched an investi-
gation into the detention of scores of Jews who were being held at Ellis
Island. As a result, the then-commissioner on the island was dismissed
and the detainees were freed.

The *Forward*, or as it was familiarly known, the *Forverts*, was more
than a voice of protest and reform, though it certainly was that. It was
gossip and amusement; it was a connection to home and family, report-
ing news from the Old Country and solving problems of adapting to the
New World. You're a *greeneh* (greenhorn) here, unused to the customs of
the land? Read about how American fathers go fishing with their sons.
Of a more serious nature, the *Forward* reported on instances of crime in
the Jewish neighborhoods. "A seventy-five-year-old man marries a twen-
ty-five-year-old girl, steals her sixty-seven dollars, and disappears. Also
has another wife."*

But the most popular feature in the newspaper was undoubtedly the
advice column. As intensely read as any Dear Abby or Ann Landers column today, these pleas to the editor for help were called the *bintel brief*
[bundles of letters]. In the *bintel brief*, laid bare for all to see—and relate
to—were the life struggles of a people dealing with poverty, romance, and
difficult personal relationships. "What can I do with my son who is getting too American and won't listen to me anymore?" a parent writes. The
words of a miserable young former Yeshiva student were compelling as he
described the conflicted relationship he had developed with "a very fine
gentile girl." What to do?

These dramas, small and large, were among the reasons why the *Forward* was a fixture in my home, as it was in every other Jewish household
that I ever heard of. Grandma Franklin never read an English-language
paper, having never learned to read English. But during the years when I
was growing up and she lived with us, it was often my daily task to run to
the corner store and buy her the *Forverts*, her link with a vital world that
was changing more rapidly than she could fathom.

---

*Howe, Irving. *World of Our Fathers*. p. 99.

VIII. The New World

America is for everyone, they say, the greatest piece of luck.
For Jews, it's a garden of Eden, a rare and precious place.

—*Sholom Aleichem*

SHOLOM ALEICHEM KNEW (after all, he was Jewish) that irony is as much a part of the Jewish psyche as it is of Jewish history and literature. He often wrote tales recounting the adventures of fools who could be wise and wise men who were fools. Surely his words of America ring with double meaning. His simple, idealistic view of this "Eden" carries a rich vein of skepticism, an implicit acknowledgment of man's folly and the quixotic nature of life.

Born Sholom Rabinowitz in Russia in 1859, this beloved Yiddish writer, whose adopted name means "peace be with you," came out of a *shtetl* in the Ukraine and eventually made his way to America in 1914. After only two years in the promised land, he died in 1916. That in itself is an irony worthy of Sholom Aleichem.

America was—and is—a "rare and precious place." Certainly it was a haven, a land that provided a home for the persecuted and poverty-stricken immigrant. But, in fact, no place on earth is a "Garden of Eden." Although in America, no one—no military or police—had indiscriminate power to come knocking at one's door, arousing terror or intruding on one's person or property, outrages of this nature have occurred on occasion. Here in Boston, a retired black clergyman recently suffered a fatal heart attack when federal agents mistakenly broke into his apartment in search of drugs. The outcry from the press, the public, and city officials showed that this kind of police action could not be tolerated.

If an immigrant expected a land where the streets were paved in gold, then surely there would have been bitter disappointment. In *The Rise of David Levinsky*, the protagonist describes his first impressions of "a great American city. Instead of stumbling upon nuggets of gold, I found signs of poverty.... I came across a poor family who...had been dispossessed for non-payment of rent.

"A mother and her two little boys were watching their pile of furniture...on the sidewalk while the passers-by were dropping coins into a saucer.... What puzzled me was ...the furniture. For in my birthplace chairs and a couch like those...would be signs of prosperity. But, then, anything was to be expected of a country where the poorest devil wore a hat and a starched collar."*

What is astonishing is how much the immigrant Jews and their descendants have achieved in this extraordinary country. Starting with nothing, a rag-tag group of people, poor and often illiterate, have risen to the top echelons of American society, excelling in every field of endeavor. Jewish Americans sit on the Supreme Court; they serve in the United States Congress. They have been the recipients of Nobel prizes in science and Pulitzer prizes in literature. They have written America's music and plays, sung the songs and filmed the movies. They have become doctors, lawyers, business people and professors, as well as painters and poets.

Certainly the German Jews who preceded the "Russians" had established a foundation for success. Witness the retail empires in New York and elsewhere. In Boston in 1881, William Filene opened a dress-trimming shop on Winter Street, a precursor to the chain of Filene's department stores. The career of a seventeen-year-old named Levi Strauss, who entered the country in 1848, is further testimony to Jewish industriousness and achievement. Could he even have imagined that 150 years later men, women, and children all over the world would be wearing his pants, his Levis?

Still, the way was hard and the road not paved with gold for those who would succeed. At the start, there may have been friendly faces—a relative already established in America who opened her apartment (what was one more mouth to feed?), or the HIAS or another Jewish welfare organization designed to ease the way for the newcomer. But the helping hand, once extended, was not to be a permanent caretaker. The immigrants had to make their own way in the new world.

And they did. They found work rolling cigars, some at home, some in shops like my Grandpa Manson. There were carpenters like Grandpa

---

*Cahan, Abraham. *The Rise of David Levinsky*. p. 95.

Franklin, building porches and houses and shops. Some peddled rags from door to door or came around the neighborhood offering to sharpen knives. They sewed clothes, bringing piecework home at night where the whole family worked on them. Others sold fruit from pushcarts in the street. They did what they had to do.

Still, there were some things they would not do. Jewish immigrants did not work as servants. They would not be maids; they would not clean other people's homes or care for other people's children. As Stephen Birmingham writes in *The Rest of Us*, "Immigrant Italians, Irish, and Swedes lined up for jobs helping to dig the tunnels for New York's subway system and lay its tracks; not the Jews...." Jews generally did not seek public jobs in the police or fire departments.

What was it that kept them from these public or private servant jobs? So long subservient, there must have been an inherent distaste for such positions. Furthermore, to don a uniform would have been abhorrent to a Jew. The memory of rampaging Cossacks wearing official uniforms, symbols of a murderous government, was a bitter memory that the New World Jew retained.

Perhaps there were other reasons as well. Surely the issues of pride and education must be considered. Jews, long called the "People of the Book" because of their devotion to the study of the Bible, had always revered knowledge. Men of learning and scholarship—the rabbis—were most admired in Jewish society. But in America, with its free schooling, education was not something just for the learned rabbis. Education was for all, especially for children. In 1908, when Jews accounted for only two percent of the population, they made up over eight percent of college students. "Today some eighty percent of America's Jews have been to college, and half of those hold advanced degrees."*

Educated people are not servile people. And they are people of some pride. There may even be a touch of arrogance in that pride. A family lives in a tenement building served by only one common toilet? A man struggles at his menial labors barely able to earn enough to survive? But he does survive, even thrive. In order to do this, he must have hope and pride and enough arrogance to believe that he is better than the peddler he is, and that his efforts—and time—will prove it.

For an incredible number of immigrant Jews, time did bring confirmation of their worth. A woman is a pushcart peddler on New York's lower East Side. Her son, Jacob Javits, will become the United States Senator from New York, serving with distinction for many years.

*Muggamin, Howard. *The Jewish Americans*. p. 15.

Leonard Bernstein, the son of Russian Jews, born and raised in the Boston suburbs, will become one of America's premier musicians, a conductor and composer. His *West Side Story* will hold a permanent place in the American musical theater.

The individual achievements of other Jewish sons and daughters of immigrant families are etched in the annals of American arts, letters, science, and business. Dr. Jonas Salk discovered the polio vaccine. Helena Rubenstein and Estee Lauder each founded a cosmetics empire. Irving Berlin wrote *God Bless America* and *White Christmas*, and George Gershwin, the musical genius, wrote such timeless songs as *Embraceable You* as well as to *An American in Paris* and the opera *Porgy and Bess*.

There are singers such as Bob Dylan (Robert Zimmerman), Simon and Garfunkel, and Beverly Sills (Belle Silverman), the renowned opera diva. There are an incredible number of comedians, including Eddie Cantor, Milton Berle, Jack Benny, George Burns, Lenny Bruce, Billy Crystal, Joan Rivers, Roseanne, Sid Caesar, Carl Reiner, Mel Brooks, Alan King, Jerry Lewis, the incomparable Marx Brothers and, yes, even the Three Stooges. The birth names of Moe, Curly, and Shemp were Moses, Jerome, and Shemp Horowitz; Larry, who joined the group later, was born Louis Feinberg.

The illustrious roster goes on to include actors Kirk Douglas, Lauren Bacall, Richard Dreyfuss, Goldie Hawn, Dustin Hoffman, Walter Matthau, Bette Midler, and writer/actor/director Woody Allen. The moguls, the Jewish men who helped create Hollywood, were Samuel Goldwyn, Louis B. Mayer, Harry Cohn, and David O. Selznick.

Radio and television pioneers included David Sarnoff and William Paley. Among accomplished Jewish artists are writer and screen director Nora Ephron and directors Billy Wilder and Mike Nichols. Playwrights Lillian Hellmann and Arthur Miller created classic American dramas with *The Little Foxes* and *Death of a Salesman*, respectively. Neil Simon's singular success has meant, among other things, that he is the only contemporary playwright to have a Broadway theater named after him. Other writers include Saul Bellow, who has won the Nobel prize for literature, and Philip Roth, Norman Mailer, David Halberstam, and Cynthia Ozick. The list goes on. Though writers of a different genre, the extraordinary Friedman twins, better known as *Dear Abby* and *Ann Landers* are probably more widely—and daily—read than anyone else.

There are also those Jews who have achieved a more dubious eminence. Ivan Boesky and Michael Millken both went to jail for their white-collar crimes in the greedy 1980s. Of a more murderous bent were Meyer Lansky, Bugsy Seigel, and Arnold Rothstein. Each of these men rose to the top in his nefarious career of crime. Seigel, for example is credited with creating the desert gambling oasis of Las Vegas. However, I am understandably drawn to the story of Arnold Rothstein. As far as I know, we are not related. Described as one of the most powerful Jewish gangsters of the 1920s—sort of a triple-threat man, you might say, in the fields of gambling, boot-legging, and narcotics—he established himself as a kingpin of crime. But it was as the brains behind the Black Sox scandal of 1919 that Rothstein carved for himself a truly memorable niche in the annals of crime.

Here was a guy who actually "fixed" a World Series game. Imagine: Baseball, America's beloved pastime, a sport of heroes (at least it was then) became forever tainted because some of its players sold out for money. Lots of money. That is how the Chicago White Sox were dubbed the Black Sox.

But for most Jews, as for most people, a more honorable and respectable kind of achievement is chronicled. The opportunity for success was the magnet that propelled people to American shores. And despite the fiction of streets paved with gold, most immigrants understood full well that in order to "become someone," to "be something," one would have to make it happen. Finding a job was the beginning.

Work was hard and not well paid. At the turn of the century, a man or woman could earn five dollars a week working on shirts, making buttons and sleeves. Of a five dollar weekly salary, perhaps one and a half dollars went for rent, two dollars for food, and always a dollar was put away for savings. On Sundays one could enjoy the free entertainment of a walk along the avenue or, for pennies, the pleasure of the Yiddish theater.

There was work to be had, particularly for the many Russian Jews who had worked in the "rag trade," or the "needle trade," as the clothing business was called. At the turn of the century New England had a thriving textile business, and thus there were factory jobs for cutters and stitchers. Those who came with skills in the needle trade found work. But the work could be terrible. The term "sweatshop" was coined to describe the miserable workplace—where immigrants stitched and cut in hot and crowded conditions, working long hours for little pay.

But even the unskilled, those who were rag-men and peddlers, found work. In the 1930s, when I was a child, there were still itinerant salesmen who came around to the neighborhood selling their wares off of pushcarts. Aprons and house dresses, pots and pans were all traded in the streets of Boston. I remember an old, bearded man who pushed a cart that held a stone shield. He seemed small and bent, as if worn down by the woes of the world, yet his sing-song cry, "Knives sharpened! Knives sharpened!" had a happy lilt that carried housewives out of their homes, pulled to him as if by a magnet. The women brought him their kitchen knives to be whetted and honed on the wheel. We children gathered around to watch, delighted as sparks flew into the air when the steel of the knife met the flint of the wheel.

I also can recall the enterprising photographer who, on sunny days, would come ambling down the street leading a donkey on a rope. The city streets, lined with concrete and tenements, were an incongruous setting for the slow clip-clop of this intriguing yet indifferent creature. Like the Pied Piper of old, the photographer and his beast of burden attracted all those mothers who could not resist the appeal of memorializing their four-year-olds sitting tall in the saddle, holding the reins of a sturdy—if singularly bored—mount.

In Boston, where I grew up, there developed a large community of Jews. Chicago and Philadelphia would also become major centers of Jewish population. No city, however, compared to New York. The largest concentration of Jews settled there, particularly on the lower East Side. It is no accident that three quarters of all the Jews who landed in New York remained there. A major reason, of course, was that they couldn't afford to travel anywhere else. A David Levinsky, arriving with four cents in his pocket, would find that his opportunities for moving on were severely limited. Even the cheapest train ticket would have been beyond his reach. Today, though many can afford to move wherever they wish, New York remains home to more than a million Jews.

An interesting aspect of the Jewish experience in America was the curious—and not always successful—relationship that the Jew had with the land. Why is it that so many Jews are urban residents? Why is it that Jews have settled in the cities and not in the heartland? Why do we think of Boston and Los Angeles and not Kansas City when we think of centers of Jewish population? And yet of course there are Jews in Kansas as there are in Kentucky, Montana, and everywhere. The answers to these questions can be read in the history of the Jews. Though the Bible tells us of Jewish farmers and shepherds, more recent history shows that for centuries Jews in Europe were prohibited from owning land. Restrictive laws barred Jews from most trades except commerce. Their experience as farmers had been meager; their skills not well-developed.

Yet there are exceptions—dairy farming for one—instances where Jews have worked the land to reclaim it and make it their own. The most stunning modern-day example is in Israel, where the people have made the deserts bloom and the lands yield a cornucopia of riches.

Through the years there were other attempts to farm. American Jewish farming settlements were established by immigrants throughout the Northeast. I can remember that when I was a child in the '30s and '40s, we took Sunday rides to the "country," when we would pile into our old Chevrolet and head out to Sharon to see the chicken farms and the dairy farms. My father thought it somewhat quixotic. "Jews running a farm, for cryin' out loud!" Maybe that's why we kept going out there; perhaps he needed to see it to believe it. My father knew people who sold furniture, sold shoes, sold insurance. The thought of a Jewish farmer was almost more than he could understand.

Sharon was—and is—a small community. But something happened to the farms there that occurred on a larger scale elsewhere. Many of the farms failed. And when they failed, their owners, in order to make a living, turned their farmhouses into guesthouses and boardinghouses where tired, over-worked, city people could come to rest and enjoy the fresh country air. Some of the greatest resorts of the Catskills began in this way. In 1904 the Evergreen Farm House advertised its bucolic advantages, stating, "Elevation, 2000 feet. Baths, toilets, cold and hot water on every floor. Fresh milk, butter, and eggs from our own farm. Kosher. Five hundred fruit trees. Piano and other entertainment. Books and newspapers. Playground for children."*

In later years, resorts such as the Concord and Grossinger's would establish the standard—and the stereotype—for the sprawling Catskill hotel with its golf course, tennis courts, and swimming pool. The Concord was the largest, with over 1,200 rooms. Entertainment was always a staple ingredient of the resorts, and in the '30s and the '40s, comics and their comedy acts found a home "in the mountains."

These were places where a Jewish family could go, where they could eat, swim in the lake or the pool, eat, play cards, eat, rest, eat some more, *and* see terrific shows. It is amazing to consider the young Jewish comedians and writers who got their start performing in the Catskills. Many of them went on to become famous, many of them in the fledgling medium of television. People like Sid Caesar, Milton Berle, Mel Brooks, Red Buttons, and Buddy Hackett, to name just a few. Whether these resorts were modest or luxurious, simple or grand, they all had one thing in common: they all were Jewish resorts. Jews owned them, Jews ran them, and only Jews patronized them. This exclusively wasn't, of course, just a matter of finding comfort with one's own kind, where the food was kosher or where you knew the Blooms had vacationed last summer.

---

*Howe, Irving. *World of our Fathers.* p. 216.

These Jewish resorts had developed in part as a reaction to those places where Jews were denied access. Private country clubs and hotels often had an unstated but nonetheless official policy of excluding Jews. I can recall as a child driving past a particular club with its rolling green lawn and being told of its other attractions, the swimming pool, clubhouse, and tennis courts, all of which tantalized me with visions of riches and glamour. "Forget it," my father would say, "the place is 'restricted.'" "Restricted" was a term we all learned early on; it meant "no Jews allowed."

There is a story told about Bernard Baruch, the famous financier who was a confidante of President Franklin Roosevelt in the 1940s. Arriving in Florida in a town outside Orlando, he entered a hotel and approached the registration desk. When they saw the name Baruch, they told him that there was no room. As Mr. Baruch prepared to leave, the hotel personnel suddenly realized who he was. There'd been a mistake, they said; of course there was room for him. Mr. Baruch continued on his way out of the hotel saying, "You didn't make the mistake. I did."

Discrimination doesn't take a holiday. Signs that said "Christian Only" were plain enough to see. "No Jews or dogs allowed" read the sign posted at a Maryland beach. Yet sometimes the signs were invisible but still easy to discern. And you didn't have to go on vacation to find them. In real estate, before the enactment of anti-discrimination laws, landlords could refuse to rent or sell to Jews. There were all sorts of ways to practice discrimination, subtle ways. A Mrs. Wilson might inquire about an apartment to rent and receive courteous answers to her questions. But should Mrs. Goldberg call to see the place, she would be told, "Sorry, it has been rented."

Anti-Semitism was, unfortunately, alive and well in other places too. It is sad that in this great country, where Jews enjoyed more freedom than anywhere else, absolute freedom was not absolutely the case. If the *goyim* didn't want you in their fancy clubs, you could start your own. It they didn't rent to you, you could find another apartment. But if they didn't want you in their offices or colleges....

Job discrimination was established through many signs that read "Christians only need apply." The struggle for higher learning was exacerbated for Jews by the quota system in force at many of America's colleges and universities. Education was always a primary focus and goal for the Jew. To be shut out of temples of learning because of one's religion was a terrible thing. Between 1920 and 1922 Columbia University, in its effort to keep its Jewish student population down, instituted regional quotas. Since most Jewish applicants were from the East, this policy had the effect of cutting the percentage of Jewish students from forty to twenty-two percent. "By the mid-twenties it was common knowledge that quotas regarding Jews had been established at the prestige universities in the East."*

*Howe, Irving. *World of Our Fathers*. pp. 411-412.

IX. The Family

A Jewish mother was asked the ages of her two children.
"Why," she said, "the doctor is two and the lawyer is three."

IN 1900, MY GRANDPARENTS Wolf and Jennie Frumkin—already the parents of six children including my mother, who had just been born—were living at 12 Barton Street in Boston's West End, an immigrant neighborhood of working-class Jews.

In 1910 the West End was home to 24,000 Jews, the largest concentration of Eastern European Jews in the city. It is there that writer Mary Antin and her family lived when they came to America, and she described it in her book, *The Promised Land* as "the wrong end of the city...the slums of Boston." But her words were without rancor since, despite the mean and lowly tenement district she lived in, Antin felt herself fortunate to be in Boston, in America, the land of the free.

Many years later, as a newlywed in 1953, I too felt fortunate to be living in the West End, on Phillips Street. Yet I too heard it described as "the wrong end" of the city, this time by my mother. Genuinely chagrined as we proudly showed off our two-room apartment with its closet-sized kitchen and bedroom window that looked out onto an alley, she cried, "How could you do this? It took us years, a generation, to get out of the West End, and now you come back!"

Whereas I viewed my move to Boston as romantic, even Bohemian, my mother believed I was jeopardizing the advances made by our family. Because there I was, right back where she had started from. Though I believe she was mistaken, I understand far better now than I did then how my mother would be concerned about our living situation. After all, she had been motivated all her life by the desire of the immigrant family to improve its lot in life. The parents might be poor, they might be ignorant, but they certainly knew what they wanted for their children: a better life.

And education was the key, the passport, the way out and the way up in the Promised Land.

To add to the marvels of the American educational system, the public schools were free. No more scrimping and saving to see that the children could go to school. No longer would parents be faced with the terrible choice of deciding which of their children would receive an education, since a family couldn't afford to send all the children to school. In America, everyone, rich or poor, had the same opportunity. Not only was education free, it was compulsory. Children were *expected* to go to school. It was nothing less than a miracle.

Writing in *The Promised Land*, Mary Antin told about her second day in America and being "thrilled with the realization of what this freedom of education meant. A little girl from across the alley came and offered to conduct us to school.... This child, who had never seen us till yesterday, who could not pronounce our names, who was much better dressed than we, was able to offer us the freedom of the schools of Boston! No application made, no questions asked, no examinations, rulings, exclusions; no machinations, no fees. The doors stood open for every one of us. The smallest child could show us the way."*

The never-ending wonder of free, compulsory education carried an extra benefit for the immigrant family. It wasn't just what the children would learn; it was what they wouldn't learn. The children would be taught history and mathematics; they would study the books of the world's best writers; in science they would learn about the properties of metals and the aspects of the natural world. But they would not be taught or indoctrinated in or forced to practice any religious precepts.

Immigrant parents might have been unfamiliar with the founding fathers or unable to name Washington, Adams, or Jefferson; in all likelihood they had never read the Constitution nor heard the phrase "separation of church and state." But as their children went off to school to learn their ABCs, the parents too were learning more about what it meant to be an American. In America, Catholic, Protestant, and Jew were free to go to their respective places of worship. And in school they would sit side by side and together learn how to read, how to do multiplication, and learn how the American Revolution was fought and won. For immigrant families, this was truly wonderful.

There was, however, another form of education going on beside that being received in the classroom. These were the lessons of the street. The Jewish child might be learning English in school, on the street she was

*Antin, Mary. *The Promised Land*. p. 186.

Barton Street, West End, Boston, 1910

picking up slang. "How to speak American" and "how to dress American" were as much a part of the daily curriculum as the ABCs.

Adults were learning American ways too. The men forsook their long black frock coats and cut off their sidelocks, the long sideburn curls worn by the devout Jew. And the wig, a symbol of the orthodox Jewish woman, was also discarded. To look like a "greenhorn," someone fresh off the boat, was humiliating. Everyone was in a hurry to adopt American styles, language, and dress. Even the names were changed: Fruma became Frances, Yossel became Joseph. Learning how to be Americans was another lesson in freedom. In the Old Country, since Jews were not permitted to participate fully in the larger life of the community, their own traditions and folkways had flourished within their tight little world. In the *shtetl* everyone lived the same, observing holidays and the Sabbath.

But in America, the Jew was being assimilated into the larger community, and it was harder to maintain the old traditions. Jewishness, or *Yiddishkeit*, was in danger of being diluted or lost. *"Amerikane kinder* (American children)!" was the lament of the Jewish father as his sons stopped going to synagogue, preferring to play in the streets on a Saturday with friends. And as parents continued to speak Yiddish to their children, only to be answered in English, a new proverb was coined: "In America the child brings up the parents."

In 1900, my grandmother Jennie Frumkin was thirty-six, Wolf was forty-two, and they had six children. Shmuel, who later became Charlie, was fifteen; Lizzie, who became Betty, was thirteen; and Max, who became Warren, was ten. Uncle George was three, Uncle Morris was two, and my mother, Frances, was an infant, born in January, the first month of the first year of the new century. Growing up, there was never any problem for me in remembering my mother's age. Just think of what year it is," she'd tell me, "and that's how old I am."

Following the paper trail through the United States Census and other sources, I have been able to determine much of this information, despite the inaccuracies. Why, I wondered, is Grandpa listed as being forty-two in 1900 and only forty-four in 1910? One clue comes from a current newspaper article about New York's newest immigrant families.

"Immigrant parents are easily put off by any kind of request for information.... They're fearful of the government [and] they're afraid...of even giving out their mailing address."* Intimidation, confusion, inability to understand English—all these factors contributed to inconsistencies in data. It also shows us that whether it's 1900 or 1992, nothing changes.

The New York Times. Nov 7, 1992. p. 25.

Warren, infected with incurable wanderlust, was a rebel who left home early and often. He always came back, but not until he had managed to sail off on some ship heading somewhere—anywhere. He might sign on to crew for some wealthy person or perhaps work as a chauffeur. He didn't care. Even later, as a married father of two, as his daughter Lucille remembers, he and his wife had an argument and Warren got into the car to drive and cool off. But Warren, being Warren, didn't just drive around Boston a little. He drove to California.

Aunt Betty states in the 1910 census that she was employed as a "dry goods saleswoman." A true original, and eccentric, Betty was unlike anyone else in the family. And I was entranced by her. She always believed that she had some telepathic powers, and though others in the family might scoff, they tended to listen when Betty would wake up in the morning having dreamt about her errant brother Warren and announce, "Warren's coming home today."

And indeed, there he would be, after having been away for six months without having sent home any word at all. Betty was not ordinary; she proved it again when she married George Barton.

Betty worked at a sewing machine for a company called Brown & Durrell. She caught the eye of the young man who drove the delivery truck up from New York to Boston. He was handsome and dashing. He was something else too. Not Jewish. In 1912, Betty and George were married. Betty moved to New York and had two children, Harold, born in 1913, and Frances, born in 1915. In 1918, the year the First World War ended, tragedy struck. Betty, thirty-one years old, became a widow. George Barton succumbed to the influenza epidemic, which killed an estimated twenty million people worldwide, more than 500,000 of them Americans.

Though the phrase had not yet been invented, Betty was learning how difficult it could be to be a "single mother" trying to raise two children. At some point she was running a boarding house in New York, and family lore would have it that it was perhaps more—or less—than it seemed: a boarding house of ill repute. That certainly may have had something to do with the fact that it was deemed an inappropriate place in which to raise a young girl. Frances was sent up to Boston to live with the Franklins.

My mother, indeed all of the family, always considered Frances not so much a niece as a younger sister. But eventually Frances went back to New York. Betty had married again. Morty Weil could not have been more unlike George Barton. Morty was a gambler who never worked a day in his life. Said to be a prototype for one of writer Damon Runyon's

Broadway characters, Uncle Morty hung out at Lindy's, the famous New York restaurant of the '40s, cigar clenched in his teeth, discussing horse racing with other like-minded gentlemen. Morty may have been a little rough around the edges, but he was warm and funny. Described by his grandson Kenneth Barton as a "soft touch," Morty was at home in the streets of New York, where he seemed to know everyone.

"Hey, kid, how ya doin'?" was Morty's habitual greeting. Whether it was to the races or Coney Island or the corner newsstand, Ken recalls trotting happily off with Morty. Morty was, of course, as politically incorrect as it was possible to be. "Hey, Chico, how ya doin'?" was his way of saying hello to anyone not of Caucasian origin.

I came from a family whose members were sober citizens who got up and went to the office or the store every day except Sunday, and you can imagine the effect on me of such a colorful character. Going to visit Aunt Betty and Uncle Morty in New York was always an exciting event, not only because of how different they were from everyone else in the family, but because it was New York. Boston was a fine place to be from, but "life" and "living," I was convinced, were happening in New York.

In front of Aunt Betty's and Uncle Morty's apartment stood a doorman resplendent in uniform, epaulets and fringe adorning his marvelous coat. In Boston, the only place I'd ever seen such a sight was in front of the grandest of Boston hotels, the Ritz-Carlton, overlooking the Public Garden. Betty seemed to me to be a creature from another world. She went to the races with Morty. She dyed her hair. She was a little ditzy, sort of distracted when she talked. She lied about her age. In short, she was quite marvelous.

Frances always remained close to her Boston roots; as adults, we cousins have maintained those ties. Of her brother Harold, though, I have no real memories. There was a photo of him however, that was unforgettable. He was a handsome, dark-haired navy pilot climbing into his World War II plane, looking confident and dashing as he prepared to go off and do battle with the enemy. Harold was shot down somewhere over the Pacific in 1944, leaving behind his wife Natalie, and their four-year-old son, Kenneth.

Betty never got over the loss of her son. She dreamed about Harold and throughout her life maintained the belief that he was alive somewhere, perhaps on a desert island, and would be found and returned to her. If Betty and Warren were the rebels of the Franklin family, my father's brother Ned held the same distinction in the Manson clan. I never knew him, but I wish I had. I remembered once how my father, shaking his head, referred to his brother Ned as a "puzzle," saying, "he wasn't like the rest of us."

Apparently Dad was right. More so than I ever realized. Only recently I was enlightened by my cousin Bob Greenglass, who remembers Ned well. Twelve years older than I, Bob recalls that Ned "was the kind of uncle anyone would want," describing a "swashbuckling idealist, the kind of guy who came and went, always off on different adventures." Bob says that he believes Ned was a communist, and that in later life he was addicted to drugs. Bob understands that Ned was sickly through much of those years and was devotedly nursed by his wife until his death in New York City.

Ned's path was dramatically different, separating him from a family that was far more traditional, even conventional. Most of my uncles worked at white-collar jobs; they sold insurance or shoes or, like my father, refrigerators and stoves at Jordan Marsh Company. Uncle Murray was in "butter and eggs," a broker in those commodities.

My mother's brothers were all hardworking. Uncle Arthur owned a hardware store. Like his father, he knew tools. And George also took after his father, becoming a carpenter. My memory of Charlie is that he owned a corner variety store, a place where I was allowed to pick out candy or a comic book for free. Naturally, I thought that occupation was of the highest order and that he alone, of all my mother's six brothers, must certainly be the most successful and admired.

Neither my parents nor any of their siblings ever attended college. They all did finish high school, however, which was unusual for those times. The women worked as sales clerks and secretaries. My mother used to speak nostalgically of her work as a secretary at the Massachusetts State House, a job she held for many years, from 1918 to 1933. My father, before becoming a salesman, worked as a court stenographer. Though this job required real skill, it was silent, solitary work and could not have been a comfortable fit for such a genial and outgoing man. My relatives found themselves the same kinds of positions in the work world as did thousands of other members of the Boston Jewish immigrant community. Many people opened small shops or groceries, some of which specialized in Jewish foods.

In detailing the kinds of vocations open to the immigrant Jew, one book says that "the more educated worked as cigar makers, which was considered an 'intelligent' occupation."* It's an appealing description, one I can't help but like as I picture my Grandpa Manson bent over his work,

*Isaac M. Fein. *Boston—Where it All Began*. p. 48.

folding and unwrapping tobacco leaves, making cigars. But I don't know. The truth is that the quiet man who was my grandfather didn't give many clues as to intelligence, humor, or nature. The truth is I never knew him.

I don't even know whether Grandpa smoked the cigars he made. But my father did. He loved his El Productos. He relished his smokes almost as much as mother disliked them. He smoked for over thirty years, into middle age, until, concerned about his health, he suddenly quit one day, never to smoke again. My mother was vastly relieved. She had been going around the house for years sniffing her displeasure, emptying out overflowing ashtrays into a little covered metal hand-held trash-holder called a "silent butler."

After giving up his beloved stogies, it seems to me, the only vice my father retained was that of playing cards. He and my mother played cribbage, canasta, and double solitaire. He played bridge or poker or pinochle when they got together with their friends or my mother's sisters and their husbands. He loved all those games.

He also loved comedians and musical acts. He'd grown up with vaudeville and used to recount to me his delight in seeing Sir Harry Lauder during his appearances at the Metropolitan Theatre in Boston (now the Wang Center). Never having seen the beloved Scotsman, I had no idea of his particular charms. "Oh, he could make you laugh!" my father would say. "And he sang such songs." Years later, when vaudeville was staging something of a comeback, I felt pretty much the same way about seeing Danny Kaye at the very same theater.

My father had his own little act, a special remedy for hiccups. I never knew anyone but my dad to do it, and I have no idea how it originated. But I thought it was both brave and crazy. When the uncontrollable spasms would come over him, he would march resolutely into the kitchen, go to the cabinet, and take down the bottle of vinegar. Pouring a full tablespoon of the stuff, he would swallow it down manfully, sigh deeply, and smile with satisfaction. No more hiccups. He never understood why everyone didn't do it.

X. Boston and Brookline

Remember, remember always, that all of us...are descended from immigrants....

—*President Franklin D. Roosevelt, 1938*

BOSTON AT THE TURN OF THE CENTURY was a city at odds with itself. Like much of America, change and growth were in the air, as exemplified by the explosion of immigration. In 1850, the population of Boston was 136,000. In 1873, the Jewish population of the city was 2,500. By 1900, the first year of the new century—the year my mother was born—Boston had grown to 560,000 people, and with the influx of Eastern European immigrants during the 1880s and 1890s, the Jewish population of Boston had mushroomed to 40,000.*

There had always been a small but distinct Jewish presence in America. The oldest synagogue in the United States, located in Newport, Rhode Island, dates from 1763. On the eve of the American Revolution, in 1775, there were about 1,000 Jews in the colonies. A number of these Jews, like Isaac Moses, who loaned money to the incipient American government, achieved prominence.

After 1840, the Jewish population increased. The immigrant explosion was still far off, when the latter part of the century would bring two million Eastern European Jews to these shores. But in the 1840s the German Jews started to arrive. It wasn't long after that that Boston had its first Jewish congregation.

In 1846 Ohabei Shalom [Lovers of Peace] was established with forty people. Along with it came a Hebrew school, a cemetery, and two

---

*Sarna and Smith. *The Jews of Boston*. pp. 6, 329.

78

charitable associations. By 1852 a 500-seat wooden synagogue was situated on what is now Warrenton Street in Boston. However, cultural divides occurred, causing a split in the congregation. One group introduced services in English as well as other "reform" measures and left to start their own temple, later known as Temple Israel. Yet another ideological split occurred in 1858, and twelve members left to start their own congregation, Mishkan Tefila. Today all three temples are in Brookline and Chestnut Hill, Ohabei Shalom having moved in the 1920s.

In 1900 the life expectancy for men and women was forty-nine years. Wilbur and Orville Wright entered the record books with their first successful airplane flight. That year would also see the beginning of mass-produced automobiles by the Ford Motor Company. By 1910, half a million cars would be registered to Americans. The landscape was changing; new roads had to be built as new businesses emerged. Someone had to sell the cars, service them, and sell gas to keep them running.

The huge number of immigrants flooding into the United States constituted a major workforce. It was the immigrant worker who built the railroads, the roads, and the ships. It was the immigrant who toiled in factories, making shoes, stitching garments. By the late nineteenth century, the manufacture of ready-to-wear clothing had become a booming business in this country. The army of immigrant workers was helping to build America.

Besides the factories, where hours were long and pay was short, immigrant workers toiled away in "sweatshops," where working conditions could be intolerable. It is easy to understand why the name sweatshop came to identify the crammed, hot, and miserable workspaces housed in city tenement buildings. In those unforgiving places the new immigrants who had worked in the needle trade in the Old Country labored in the garment industry, stitching and cutting from early morning into the evening hours, putting in a twelve-hour day or more. Workers could be fined for using the toilet, fined for talking on the job.

A 1906 letter writer to the *Bintel Brief* states, "We work in a Bleecker Street shop, where we make raincoats. With us is a thirteen-year-old boy who works hard for the two and a half dollars a week he earns.... The boy came to work ten minutes late [one day], and the bosses docked him two cents. Isn't that a bitter joke?"*

These terrible working conditions were dictated by unscrupulous employers who took advantage of a workforce that was skilled, cheap, and vulnerable. Immigrants who could barely speak English, who were poor

---

*Metzger, Isaac. *A Bintel Brief.* p. 59.

and in desperate need of work, would take whatever employment they could find. They were expected to work six days a week, sometimes more. Workers were often confronted by harassment, even in the form of an intimidating sign hung in the workplace reading "If you don't come in on Sunday, don't come in on Monday."

It would not be long before the progressive reform spirit would rise in revolt against the miserable working conditions and the abusive employers who imposed them. And nothing ignited the reform labor movement as much as the fire at the Triangle shirtwaist company in 1911.

In less than twenty minutes, as fire raged through the New York tenement building that housed the overcrowded sweatshop company, 147 workers died. Many burned to death; many jumped to their deaths from the eighth, ninth or tenth floor, floors that could not be reached by fire wagons whose ladders only extended to the seventh floor.

In the wake of this tragedy, thousands of people turned out for the funeral march. Workers marched and protested and organized, fighting for laws that would grant safety in the workplace, reasonable wages, and decent working conditions.

However, though it has been a century since exploitive labor practices were first reported and though laws have been passed to strike down these practices, they have not been eliminated. *The New York Times* of February 6, 1995, reported in a front-page story that perhaps as many as 2,000 sweatshops still existed in New York State, citing that in one of them "a forty-four-year-old immigrant from China works twelve hours a day, seven days a week, in a windowless garment shop in Sunset Park Brooklyn, earning $200 on a good week—or less than $2.50 an hour."

And on September 13, 1995, United States Labor Secretary Robert Reich commented on "slave labor" conditions in the majority of the nation's 20,000 fabric cutting and sewing shops, saying it was "as bad as it was at the beginning of the century."

Such divisions among urban dwellers, between workers and bosses, rich and poor, were never more evident than in Boston in 1900. There were the Brahmins of Back Bay, the wealthy Yankees who, it seemed, had always been here. And increasingly there were workers, mostly immigrants, who lived in the low-income areas. From 1870 to 1900, Boston's neighborhoods of Roxbury, Dorchester, and West Roxbury grew from 60,000 to 227,000.*

My father's people lived in East Boston, and my mother's people first settled in the city's West End, which in 1900 was the city's largest Jewish

*Warner, Sam B. *Streetcar Suburbs.*

Community, just as the Lower East Side was in New York or the West Side in Chicago. The buildings were crowded tenements where there was usually one toilet to a building. People took in boarders to ease the financial burden. Large families occupied flats, families of six, eight, or more children. The apartments were usually without hot water, hence the name "cold-water flat."

Synagogues, Jewish shops and even a *mikveh* were part of the mosaic of immigrant life in a neighborhood where Jews, Italians, and Irish all lived side by side. The dominance of the Boston Brahmin was receding. Relations among the different immigrant groups were sometimes strained. Jewish boys of that era would recount their harrowing journeys back and forth to Hebrew school, a route made tortuous by the frequent taunts and beatings they would receive at the hands of neighborhood Irish boys.

Later many Jews moved south to the area of Blue Hill Avenue—known pejoratively as "Jew Hill Avenue"—which consisted of Dorchester, Mattapan, and Roxbury. In these neighborhoods of Boston, in addition to apartments, there were single-family houses; there were two-decker and three-decker wooden buildings too. And a little bit of grass too.

Roxbury is where my parents went to live when they married in 1927. In that year, Boston's population was 790,000; eleven percent, or 90,000, of them were Jews. It is in that nexus of Jewish population around Blue Hill Avenue that some of my earliest memories are anchored. Franklin Park and the zoo. Rollerskating on the sidewalk. Goldfish and a pet turtle, the only pets deemed appropriate for an apartment-dwelling child. A hot summer's afternoon and the interminable wait for the ice cream wagon. Another day, the sun beats warm on my bare legs as I sit in a stroller holding my pail and shovel. My mother is taking me to the sandbox in the park. I was only three; can I really remember this scene, even the color of the pail? Red. Or is it the photograph in the family album that provides me with instant recall?

Later, in 1939, when I was five, we lived in an apartment on Crawford Street in Roxbury, a neighborhood that was part of a large and vital Jewish community. My Grandma and Grandpa Manson lived in a first-floor apartment on Intervale Street. My father's brother, my Uncle Billy, and his family lived in a single-family house in Mattapan and were therefore rich, as I believed. Aunt Helen, my mother's sister, lived just blocks away from us, and all my parents' friends—the Udelsons, Rose Abrams, the Komins—were in the neighborhood.

On Blue Hill Avenue you could find practically anything you wanted.

Of course, you still went downtown to Jordan Marsh for clothes or furniture—or you got it wholesale from your uncle's brother-in-law. But Blue Hill Avenue had the candy stores and delicatessens, the butcher shops, bakeries, and drugstores. Here was the glamorous and opulent Morton Theatre, the movie house with the painted clouds and blinking stars in the ceiling, as grand as any film ever projected on its screen.

Here too on Blue Hill Avenue was the famous "G&G," the deli named for its owners, Irving Green and Charlie Goldstein. Noted as much for its congeniality as for its corned beef, the G&G became a legend, a popular gathering place for locals and politicians.

The G&G was the one campaign stop in the area that no politician, local or national, dared bypass. Eager to win the Jewish vote, candidates from state representative to president, including John F. Kennedy, came to press the flesh and nosh on a pastrami sandwich.

After several years of nursery school at the Hecht House (the Jewish Community Center), I started first grade at William Lloyd Garrison School in 1940. The swirl of memories brings back images of a concrete playground, a girl I hated named Marsha, and blond-haired Bobby Hurwitz, whom I loved. I remember penmanship and the Palmer Method.

We practiced our "longhand," our writing, endlessly. The Palmer Method was invented exclusively, as we six-year-olds believed, to torture us as we sat drawing circles and lines within the ruled borders to help us develop proper legible and handsome writing. Funny thing is, most of us did.

You put your wet boots and hung your winter coat or spring jacket in the "cloak room." Your boots—or overshoes, as they were called—were aptly-named boots that were worn over your shoes.

I remember the dreaded QUARANTINE sign that hung on a door or in a window, announcing the presence of scarlet fever in the household. In those days before antibiotics, scarlet fever was a serious illness. My own bout with the disease was mild, I believe. All I remember of it was a lovely stand-up cardboard grocery store game with little cardboard people I could move around as I sat in bed, propped up by pillows. It was a gift from my father, and I loved it.

However, because of the highly contagious nature of the illness, I suffered a terrible loss after my recovery when my father, in keeping with the health rules of the time, went up to the roof of our apartment building, built a fire, and consigned to it all my germ-laden items such as washcloths, bedclothes, books, and my beloved cardboard grocery store with all its little stand-up people.

.

I remember jelly beans melting in my sweaty palm as I hurried home from school to show them to my mother—sweet, if sticky, tributes from a second-grade teacher to reward good students.

We moved from Roxbury in 1941, the year America entered World War II. Following the migratory pattern of so many of the city's Jews, we moved to an apartment in Brookline, preceded by my Aunt Bessie and her family, who lived a block away. By moving out we moved up, for Brookline, though only a few short miles away, was in fact a world apart.

"It was a clean, beautiful town," said one Jewish Brookline resident, "bucolic splendor, green grass. The public schools were like private schools. We had French in the sixth grade. They didn't have that in Roxbury or other places. It was stepping up to a prestigious place."*

To a seven-year-old, none of that mattered very much, of course. I had very little awareness of, and even less interest in, the fact that I was part of a cultural movement, a Jewish exodus to the suburbs in search of a better life. I thought I already had a good life at the Garrison School.

I didn't know about others who were sharing the same migratory pattern, nor would it have mattered to me. For example, I didn't know that before he became Leonard Bernstein, the future composer-conductor was just Lenny Bernstein, also of the Garrison School. I didn't know either that the Brookline school I would be entering had been attended by a boy named John Fitzgerald Kennedy.

In the middle of the second grade, when I entered Brookline's Edward Devotion School—named after one of the town's colonial founding fathers —I was unaware of how "prestigious" my new surroundings were. What I was most acutely aware of—and afraid of—was that I didn't know anybody, would never know anybody, and would be friendless the rest of my natural and miserable life.

There I was, a shy seven-year-old girl, standing to the sidelines on the school playground at recess and feeling terribly alone. Then a dark-blond little seven-year-old boy with gray-blue eyes fringed in dark lashes walked over to me and with five magic words—"What's your name, little girl?"—made me feel that maybe I wouldn't be doomed to a lonely purgatory after all. Robert Wool has been my dear friend ever since that day more than fifty years ago.

The original Devotion House (built around 1740) fronted the school on Harvard Street, as it does to this day. Only five miles from Boston, the town has grown from its rural, colonial beginnings to a largely urban area

---

*Phillips, Bruce. *Acculturation, Group Survival and the Ethnic Communities*. p. 82

of 55,000. The schools and street names, such as Lawrence and Driscoll, Lee and Gardner, Griggs and Corey, all attest to the town's Yankee origins.

Brookline—a much tonier name than its original seventeenth-century appellation, Muddy River—is a town of much diversity. It wasn't always that way. In 1920 there were only about 1,000 Jews in Brookline. But that was changing. In 1925, when the rabbi of the Crawford Street synagogue resigned to become the first rabbi of Brookline's Kehillath Israel, it was noted by one of his followers that "while Roxbury should lament his leaving, it should rejoice over the fact that he is only going over to Brookline, as all progressive Jews seem to be doing."[*]

When my family moved to town in 1941, the Jewish population numbered about 14,000. Today the Jewish presence is firmly established. Of 53,000 citizens, almost half—about 20,000—are Jewish.[†] Brookline is home to some of Boston's most important Jewish institutions. There are synagogues and schools. Hebrew College and the Maimonides School, one of the largest Orthodox day schools in America, are at home here. Jewish bookstores, kosher butchers, bakeries, and restaurants are all found on Harvard Street, giving the neighborhood a vibrant ethnic flavor.

Change is always occurring. Today the new immigrants, Russians and Asians, are a growing part of the Brookline community, and you can hear a smattering of international tongues as you pass people on the streets at Coolidge Corner, Washington Square, and in the Village. Town restaurants tell their own tale of diversity. Today a hungry pilgrim in Brookline can get deli or sushi, Chinese, Thai, or Cambodian. If it's Mexican or Middle-Eastern you want, you can find that too. Also Italian, Greek, and Indian. Even McDonald's.

This is a town of million-dollar estates and of public housing. Half the buildings in Brookline were built before 1939. There's a municipal golf course; there's Longwood Cricket Club, where they actually play tennis, and there's The Country Club out on Lee Street. Yes, *The* Country Club; that's what it's called and that's how it's known.

While there are many parks throughout the town, much of Brookline maintains a distinctly urban character. Along with 4,500 single-family homes, there are 20,000 apartments and condominiums. Apartment buildings sprang up around the turn of the century, when they were

---

[*]Sarna, Jonathan D. & Smith, Ellen. *The Jews of Boston.* p. 149.
[†]Israel, Sherry. *1995 CJP Demographic Study.* p. 5.

known as "French flats." And in the 1920s, because even then there were young marrieds and older retired people coming to Brookline, an apartment building like Longwood Towers was said to be home to the "newly wed and the nearly dead."

You can hop on the Beacon Street trolley at Coolidge Corner and be in Boston in minutes. Brookline is a town where registered Democrats outnumber Republicans five to one. It is the birthplace of one president, John F. Kennedy, and of 1988's presidential candidate, Michael S. Dukakis, my 1951 Brookline High classmate. (When Michael was elected governor of Massachusetts, I asked him if I might have my old job back in his new administration. In our senior year of high school, we served as officers of the Student Council, where Michael was president and I held the position of corresponding secretary. The governor, never much given to political patronage, was not swayed by my appeal.)

Brookline has also been home to many other prominent citizens throughout the years. The great architect H.H. Richardson, who designed Copley Square's Trinity Church, lived here. So did King Gillette, of razor blade fame. Poet Amy Lowell's home was in Brookline. Arthur Fiedler, of the Boston Pops lived in a Fisher Hill mansion; and Serge Koussevitsky, of the Boston Symphony, lived at the Stoneholm apartments on Beacon Street. Renowned tenor Roland Hayes made his home in Brookline; his daughter Afrika was my classmate.

Pulitzer-prize winning *Boston Globe* columnist Ellen Goodman lives here. Mike Wallace graduated from Brookline High; so did Conan O'Brien and Kennedy presidential aide Richard Goodwin. (His brother, Judge Herbert Goodwin, sits on the Brookline bench.) Barbara Walters and Leonard Bernstein lived here. Earlier residents of some renown include the father of landscape architecture in this country, Frederick Law Olmsted. Olmsted was the designer of Boston's park system, known as the Emerald Necklace, and of New York City's Central Park, and his home on Warren Street is a national historic site.

Brookline has long enjoyed the reputation of a "favored town." That was the title of an 1897 history of the town by Charles K. Bolton. Another historical study of the town written in 1898 by James Locke, was called *Ideal Suburb* and stated that Brookline was "the richest town in the United States, with an annual income greater than the whole state of New Hampshire." Indeed, many locals used the appellation "wealthy towners," to the point where our high school football team was known by that name and the local newspaper headlines would proclaim "Wealthy Towners' defeat Newton…"

No longer can Brookline claim to be the richest town in the country, and some citizens feel that the town "ain't what she used to be." It is true that the small family drugstores have all been swallowed up by the large corporate models, and there isn't any money in the town budget anymore for sidewalk snow removal. But this streetcar suburb of Boston is still a town of good schools, well-maintained parks, and fine residential areas. At Coolidge Corner, the main commercial center of the town, Woolworth's 5&10 is gone but not forgotten. The Corner may have a more homogenized look to it today, with a Starbucks, a Gap, and a Barnes & Noble bookstore, but you can still buy a yo-yo or gum at Harvard News & Gift or go to the Coolidge, the same movie theater I went to as a kid. However, the eleven-cent admission fee I paid as an eight-year-old has certainly gone the way of the dodo.

Senior citizens hang out at McDonald's, kids on rollerblades vie for space with parents pushing baby carriages. Coolidge Corner has changed, of course. But one thing about it has remained constant: it is still a vital center where people come and shop and stroll and eat ice cream and say hello to their neighbors. You could probably make that statement about the Corner in the 1890s; you still can in the 1990s.

XI. Fannie

*The twentieth-century ideals of America have been the
ideals of the Jew for more than twenty centuries.*

—*Louis D. Brandeis*

IN THE SUMMER OF 1893, there was a polio epidemic in Boston.
Perhaps the fear of the disease is what propelled Grandfather Franklin
out of Boston and to Rhode Island.

It was in Providence that Grandpa was naturalized. He remained
healthy, safe from polio, but many years later the disease did hit the
Franklin family. It was my mother's brother Morris who was stricken. I
remember that as a child I was frightened as I listened to my uncle's
heavy step as he walked down our rugless hallway. His black shoe with its
built-up sole, a shoe made to correct the crippling effect of one leg being
shorter than the other, seemed ominous somehow to a five-year-old.

In the days before modern medicine and antibiotics, contagious dis-
eases such as polio were justifiably feared. President Franklin D.
Roosevelt, as an adult, became a victim of what was then known as Infan-
tile Paralysis. The disease crippled and killed, striking cruelly and particularly at children. It has only been since 1955 and Dr. Jonas Salk's vaccine
that medicine has gained control over the disease. Prior to that, people
were frightened. I know my mother was. She believed, as did others, that
the only protection was to avoid crowds, especially in hot weather.

Whatever his reasons for being in Providence, and however long he
stayed, Wolf Frumkin eventually returned to Massachusetts. During five
years of being separated from his wife Jennie and three young children,
he worked and saved until he had accumulated enough money to bring
his family over to America. Perhaps, like the majority of immigrants, he

had to borrow money as well to pay for the *"shiffs carte"* (steamship ticket). Perhaps he could have written the same words as did one man to the *Bintel Brief*: "The first few years here I struggled and earned barely enough to survive. Still, I saved penny by penny and finally sent steamship tickets for my wife and children, whom I had left at home."[*]

And so Jennie Frumkin came to America. We can only imagine, considering many accounts of the immigrant experience, how bewildering the sights and sounds of the New World must have seemed to her. For Jennie, like other new arrivals, would suddenly be confronted by cities and their streetcars, apartments, and electric lights, things we can assume she had never before seen.

It was 1894 when Jennie, age thirty, arrived with Charlie, Betty, and Warren, who were then eight, six, and five years of age. In making their passage to the New World, the Frumkins were like many others of their time. Over a million Jewish women and children followed husbands and fathers to America, more than any other immigrant group.

By 1900 there would be three more children added to the Frumkin family. In the 1900 census Jennie stated that she was the mother of seven children, six living. Apparently she had suffered the loss of a child. Assuming that she was having babies at two-year intervals, this loss probably occurred during the first four years of her marriage, sometime between 1882 and 1886, when Charlie was born.

George, the first Frumkin child to be born in America, arrived in 1896, followed by Morris in 1898 and my mother, Frances, in 1900. Every two years until 1908 there would be another child until there were ten in all.

Large immigrant families were commonplace in those days. They usually meant hard work, scrimping, saving, and living in small quarters. The daily grind might be an unending struggle, but one could bear it as long as there was hope and a future, a future that could be secured, it was believed, through learning and education.

My mother, Fannie, graduated from Roxbury High School with the second highest honors in the class of 1917. She was seventeen. America had just entered World War I in April and was deeply engaged in the war effort, having committed more than a million troops.

A yellowing newspaper article my mother saved describes the simplicity of the graduation attire due to wartime economy. "The class voted for the [plain] graduation gowns [of middy blouses and white skirts] and to limit the expenditure as well [to $10.00] for the whole outfit....

---

[*]Metzger, Isaac. *A Bintel Brief*. p. 136.

"The girls presented a uniform appearance in gowns of white, with white shoes and stockings. As a patriotic touch, each girl wore a red-white-and-blue ribbon.... No other touch of color was worn. No elaborate hair-dressing, no expensive jewelry, nor any play of expensive materials detracted from the fresh, girlish beauty of the graduates...."

Of all the Frumkin offspring, my mother and her sister Helen were the most studious. Bessie was certainly the most fun-loving, the one who loved to sing and dance and have a good time. All three sisters loved reading and doing crossword puzzles. Betty, the oldest sister, had her own ideas about a good time, and that included spending most days at the racetrack.

My mother also wrote. As an impressionable girl of seventeen with brothers off at war fighting for America, she penned a poem titled "The Reign of Mars." "War! Bloody War! Oh how cruel is Mars / The greedy war god from his height on high / Demands the sacrifice of the nation's youth / On the altar of lust, and avarice, and hate / The mothers of the world! Theirs is the sorrow / Theirs the bleeding heart and burning tears / Theirs the memory seared in a white hot flame / Of a broken body lying in no man's land...."

The young girl who wrote those emotional lines had a heart that cried out against the tyranny of war. Her keen sense of justice was also expressed in a cooler voice when she wrote an argument to be used in a debate on equal rights for women. "Resolved: That wages of women should not be lower than those of men performing the same service in the same occupation."

I was excited to discover this paper from my mother's early years and to learn how progressive she was. But I was depressed to know that the struggle for equal pay for equal work is still being fought eighty years after my mother wrote these words:

"...The question of equal pay for equal work resolves itself down to a fight for simple justice. Equal pay has won support wherever its arguments have been fairly presented.... When one considers that this is the twentieth century in which the struggle is being fought by the women in America, one is forced to doubt the much-valued superiority of American men in their dealings with their women....

"Work is work, no matter who accomplishes it.... I hold that salary is for service and should be measured by the service rendered. The most common and persistent of the arguments proposed by the opponents of the equal pay movement is that the man should be given a higher salary than the woman because a man has—or may have—a family to support....

"Now, if salary is to be measured by the size of the wage-earner's family, why do we give to the man whose family consists of six children the same salary we give to the man with no children? And have not women also someone dependent on them?... Has not a woman who has an invalid father and an uncle in an insane asylum the same right to consideration as a man who has a wife and son to support?

"Is it just that women should be paid less for their work? Do they receive the necessities of life for less? Are their rents and taxes less? Are their doctors' fees less? Can they live for less?

"In their work, in their expenses, in all life's obligations, their burdens are as heavy as men's. Only in their pay is there a striking and unjust difference, and it is the intolerable injustice of this which [must end]...."

Fannie Franklin was a first-generation American, an idealistic young woman whose immigrant Jewish parents had come to this country in order to live without fear of being persecuted for their religion. They found that freedom and passed it along to their daughter. But the fight for social justice never ends—not for Jews, not for Americans, not for anybody—as my mother's generation and succeeding generations would discover.

The Movschovitz family in Russia, circa 1890
(left to right) Harris, Shmuel (Samuel) Ethel, Anna

Jennie, Helen, and Fannie Franklin, 1920

William and Jennie Franklin, c. 1925

Frank and Frances Manson, May 3, 1927

Frank Manson, 1930

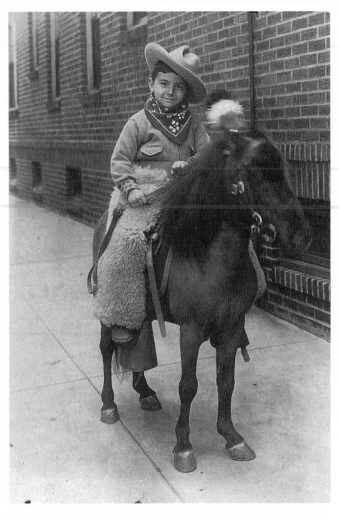

Alan Rothstein, age 4, 1934

Natalie Manson, circa 1938

Natalie (age 3 months), Grandmother Annie Manson,
and mother Frances Manson, 1934

Manson brothers and children, 1938
Natalie, Frank, Gloria, Billy, Dick, Murray

Jennie Franklin with granddaughters
Natalie Manson and Janet Parker, 1942

Alan and Natalie Rothstein, 1953

XII. Fannie and Frank

Just to be is a blessing. Just to live is holy.
—Rabbi Abraham Heschel

"MISS FRANKLIN AND MISS ABRAMS spent a week recently with friends in New York. They returned to their desks at the State House for a much-needed rest." So reads an item in the *Boston Free Press*, a newsletter for state employees that carried many lighthearted references. People's activities on and off the job were duly noted in this journal, so naturally the New York visit of two popular State House secretaries, Fannie Frankin and best friend, Rose Abrams, was cited.

It was the 1920s, and life was good in America. America had emerged from World War I victorious, but the war had taken a terrible toll. As always in war, the price is paid in blood and gold. Over 50,000 American servicemen lost their lives in the First World War, or The Great War. It was also called the war to end all wars, an appellation that would become bitterly ironic when, only twenty years later, another generation would be on the verge of yet another world war.

Armistice came in 1918, when Fannie Franklin was eighteen and Frank Manson was just twenty. In the coming decade, they would come of age and inherit a world that looked and acted vastly different from the Victorian era in which they had been born. By war's end there were between 80,000 and 90,000 Jews in Boston.*

The decade of the 1920s was an exciting, bumptious, youthful age, a time when the country seemed bent on forgetting its former solemnity and purpose in favor of fun and frolic. From Armistice Day in 1918 to

*Sarna & Smith. *The Jews of Boston.* p. 7.

the great stock market crash in 1929, Americans seeking a return to normalcy wanted to make money, live their lives, and have a good time.

The 1920s would become known variously as the Roaring Twenties and the Jazz Age. The new music, jazz, became the *leit motiv* for what seemed to many a time of reckless abandon and hedonism. F. Scott Fitzgerald, whose novel *This Side of Paradise* was published in 1920, when its author was only twenty-four, helped to characterize and label the young people—like my parents—who were coming of age. He called them—and soon others were calling them—the Lost Generation.

But like most labels, one size does not fit all. Fannie and Frank were single (they would not marry until 1927), unencumbered, and young. They were the prototypes for the Jazz Age. But their escapades were probably more innocent than those depicted by Scott Fitzgerald in his novels. And the antics of his heroes and heroines were often pretty innocent themselves.

"None of the Victorian mothers...had any idea how casually their daughters were accustomed to being kissed," Fitzgerald wrote in *This Side of Paradise*, in what passed for a shocking exposé of the time. Fitzgerald chronicles the age as one dominated by sex, jazz, drinking, and Freudian analysis. Scott Fitzgerald and his wife, Zelda, came to represent the quintessential Jazz Age couple. Glamorous and beautiful, they were self-indulgent and ultimately self-destructive.

Zelda's recklessness, her charming gaiety, became full-blown madness, and she spent much of her later years confined to a psychiatric hospital. Scott died in his 40s, an alchoholic, temporarily forgotten, his books out of print.

Alchohol took quite a toll on many of Fitzgerald's contemporaries. Because of the "evils of drink," in 1919 America decided to outlaw the production, sale, and consumption of liquor. With the enactment of Prohibition, drinking became illegal. But it did not stop.

Lots of Americans had no desire to quit drinking. In fact, they were not at all troubled by Prohibition. It represented a law that was made to be broken, and "good ole American know-how" found its ways around it. It wasn't long before the illegal manufacture and consumption of bootleg liquor became routine for many in the Roaring Twenties. This way of life lasted until Franklin Roosevelt was elected president in 1932 and Prohibition was repealed by the twenty-first Amendment to the Constitution.

Perhaps my mother was sipping "hootch" in "speakeasies" during her visits to New York; although, familiar with her lack of interest in any spirits, I somehow doubt it.

A letter from her State House colleages to my mother in New York gives news of the home front during her absence. The letter is dated 1924: "...Don't do too much shopping.... The Valentino of the office is still on the job.... Helen is not the best-looking and best-liked stenographer in the office.... If you stay away too long she may have a nervous breakdown, so be reasonable...."

Another issue of the *Boston Free Press*, of December 1923, remarks that "Fannie Frankin [is a] leading exponent of fashion. Makes a yearly trip to New York to instruct the costumers and manufacturers in what will be worn."

In reality, the hyperbolic, good-natured kidding probably meant that my mother returned home to Boston from her New York flings with a few new dresses. But, who knows? After all, it was Frances Manson I knew, my mother; I never really knew the young Fannie Franklin. I was born when she was thirty-four and growing matronly. The girl, the young woman, she had been is someone I never knew.

It is a question how much another person—even in an intimate relationship—can ever really know someone else. I am reminded of the wonderful phrase from Amy Tan's sensitive and evocative contemporary novel on mother-daughter relationships, *The Joy Luck Club*, when a mother, frustrated and hurt, shrieks out to her daughter, "You don't know me even little percent." Exactly.

With my own daughter things are the same. We enjoy the happiest of relationships—a reward, I believe, for having survived the often fractious years of her adolescence. We both laugh at the ease with which she seems able to read my mind or finish my sentences. But even to her I have said, "You know me really well, maybe even better than I think you do. But not as well as *you* think you do."

The discovery of some of my mother's papers, which I only recently came upon, illustrates just how much I didn't know and how much there was to learn about her. I was startled to discover that the words she wrote as an impressionable, idealistic sixteen-year-old girl could have been written by me. Add to that the further discovery that her passionate interests in writing and politics were exactly my own. And yet, growing up with her I was never fully aware of her passions or of our shared ambitions. (I would eventually marry on a Tuesday, unaware of the oddity and coincidence of my mother also marrying on a Tuesday.)

Yet somehow I absorbed her concern for social justice, her youthful desire to be a writer or politician. Where did her yearnings come from? Or perhaps the better question is: Where did they go? And why didn't she share them with me?

When as an eighteen-year-old I took my first job as a secretary—just like my mother—I refused to go to work in what I thought of as a routine kind of office. No law firm or insurance company for me. I wanted to work for a social agency dedicated to fighting injustice. That is how I came to work at the Anti-Defamation League of B'nai B'rith. In my mother's writings I now see her influence, but it was not something we discussed.

Also as an eighteen-year-old, in 1952, I got involved in my first political campaign. Inspired by the ideas and idealism of the Democratic nominee for president, Adlai Stevenson, I volunteered to work on his election, knocking on doors and handing out literature. This at a time when you had to be twenty-one to vote. I worked for him, I believed in him, I cried at his loss, yet I wasn't old enough to vote for him.

Again I see in my mother's writings how her passions guided me. But I can recall no strong political sentiments ever expressed by her. And both she and my father voted for Stevenson's opponent, Dwight Eisenhower.

In 1916, my mother penned a little fantasy titled "The Lady from Massachusetts" about the first woman member of Congress. Though the prospect of such an event must have seemed as remote as, say, a trip to the moon, the story was written with passion and earnestness.

"All eyes and ears were intent on the woman standing up and bravely, modestly, giving her views on the evils of child labor.... She had let it be known during her campaign that she did not want the question of [gender] to enter the minds of the voters—that she would not use that as a shield to win votes, that...she wanted them to think of her only as the representative of their interests, that she was going to Congress to help them...."

It is instructive to consider that at the time these words were penned American women were four years away from gaining the right to vote. In 1920, the nineteenth Amendment to the Constitution would finally state that "the right of citizens of the United States shall not be denied or abridged by the United States or by any State on account of sex."

Fannie also wrote lighthearted jingles and inspirational patriotic poems. At sixteen she wrote paeans to her heroes: Thomas Edison, "the genius who transformed our entire mode of living...by his creation [which has caused] the modern home to be furnished with every known device...fireless cookers, water heaters, washing machines, vacuum cleaners, reading lamps, flatirons..." and George Washington, whom she described as the "greatest name in American history."

There were other statements of freedom that my mother made. In the 1920s, when she and the century were still young, the rage was for young women to get their long hair cut off at the ear, or "bobbed." As with so many fashion statements, this one was a proclamation of freedom, youth, and independence and sounded better than it looked.

Fannie Franklin could be said to have been in the same company as F. Scott Fitzgerald's flapper, the heroine of one of his most famous stories, "Bernice Bobs Her Hair." Under the title "The Bobbies" in *The Boston Free Press* is this item: "Members: Peg Flynn, Irene Flaherty, Mildred Parsons, Helen Datow, Pauline Averett, Anna Kelley, Martha Everson, Fannie Franklin.... Rules: All members must stay in bed at least fifteen minutes longer than they did when they wore 'em long. Must donate a sum equal to the amount previously spent on hair nets to some worthy charity. Must ignore all catty remarks and take all compliments with a grain of salt.... Must never admit wishing they didn't...."

Did Fannie ever wish she hadn't cut her hair off? Or was she happy to be one of the fashionable young women of her era? She didn't embrace the fashion to the point of abandoning reason, however. She didn't smoke, as did so many other young people. Nor did she drink. She was sensible and earnest and had always seemed so to me—too much so, actually. But perhaps not as much as I thought.

Fannie went to work at the Massachusetts State House. She was proud of her job as a secretary, a job that had stiff requirements including the ability to pass a civil service test. In 1920, there were not that many career opportunities available to women. Most found themselves gravitating to traditional work as secretaries, nurses, teachers, clerks, librarians, or salesgirls. My mother worked in the Civil Service Department at the State House from 1918 to 1933, when she retired temporarily to await my birth.

Impressions in an album: The date is 1920, and there is my mother, posed with a group of girlfriends on a summer holiday at Vineyard Haven. They are wearing middy blouses and headbands. The same year, she appears in a photograph with the "Cohen girls" at the beach. My mother's dark, lustrous hair, short, but luxuriant, is in contrast to the Cohen girls, both of whom wear hats as part of their beach costumes. In one photo an unidentified man with a pipe has joined the three women. His arm is around my mother's waist; she is smiling shyly.

More photos: A 1920 picture of my mother looking very fashionable in a dark two-piece suit that flares out at the hips and has what appear to be fur cuffs. She stands with her mother, my Grandmother Jennie, a girl who looks like my Aunt Helen, who would have been twelve then. Jennie is standing erect and proud, wearing a knee-length coat over an ankle-length skirt. High-top black shoes complete the outfit. She does not seem to have a single gray hair. She was fifty-six years old.

1922: Pictures of my mother with her friends on holiday. At the beach, on picnics, with her lifelong friends Rose Abrams, Dot Udelson, and Bertha Gerber. At the state house with her friends and colleagues and sisters in crime (the other women who bobbed their hair) Anna Kelly and Pauline Averett. Wearing knickers, stockings and heels while vacationing with friends at a place called Gotz Farm in 1924.

And where was Frank Manson all this time? What was he doing? His own activities are not nearly so well documented, since there are no letters from him and very few photographs of him from that period. An early, undated photo of my father shows a handsome young man dressed in suit and bowtie, hat in hand, sitting on a stone ledge surrounding an imposing fountain. He cannot be more than twenty-two. And then he is shown in 1930, when he and my mother had been married for three years. He is holding his ubiquitous cigar, and his elegant suit is set off by a silk tie and white spats on his shoes, proper attire for a proper gentleman.

As a boy my father had been a championship runner, winning medals for his school team and for himself. My father always had in insouciant air about him. Since he was his mother's favorite child, this is not surprising. I remember feeling mildly repelled when she would tenderly lift the lid of a treasured wooden box to show me the hallowed contents. She had saved snippets of my father's hair, his baby curls. I recall looking at them with fascination, looking but not wanting to touch.

The kind of love that my grandmother gave my father must have given him the sense of confidence he always projected. Never smug or arrogant, he was the epitome of geniality, a born salesman with a teasing sense of humor.

I remember the family gatherings that were enlivened by the bantering he would exchange with his brothers-in-law Moe and Sammy, or the times in restaurants with my mother and me, when the best audience would be the innocent waitress taking our order. His bright blue eyes beaming, he'd say, "Now, I can see how nice you are; you're gonna tell me the best thing on this menu, aren't you? I certainly hope the cook is a friend of yours." My mother's response to this sort of thing was always one of supreme mortification and admonishments to "behave yourself, Frank."

He mostly did behave himself. But being easygoing didn't mean that he didn't have a temper. He did. It was hot and quick and then was gone. Yet his use of profanity was pretty mild-mannered. His favorite expletive was "for crying out loud." "What the hell," was employed with some regularity, as was "damn." But the one that upset and puzzled me was the one he would hurl at my mother during their infrequent spats. It took me a long time to realize that "quitcherbellyachin" meant "quit your belly-aching."

One of my father's earliest jobs was as a wire operator, a job several of his brothers held as well. It was an early twentieth-century inroad on the information highway. Wire operators worked as messengers, typing out data to be sent over wires. Western Union and its telegram service was the best known of these companies.

Later Dad worked as a court stenographer. But his real calling was as a salesman. In the beginning he sold shoes. He was on the road as a traveling salesman for a while and then got a job with Jordan Marsh Company, where he stayed for the rest of his working life, selling refrigerators, stoves, and other "Major Appliances." Those last two words were always capitalized in my mind.

I remember a little of his days on the road, since he occasionally took my mother and me with him. We didn't go far—New England was his territory—but driving up through Maine and New Hampshire or down to the dusty streets of Providence seemed full of romance to me, no doubt creating a lifelong desire for other roads and other places.

It's funny, but my memories of those days are all in black and white. It's like an early movie or, as one friend said in describing a family photo album prior to the time the family bought a color camera, "before the world turned to color." Everything seemed simpler, more regulated and orderly. There were things you could count on—particularly, I thought, in the world of grown-ups.

For example, everybody wore hats. The unspoken dress code was fairly strict in the thirties and forties. By word and deed, my mother taught me that nice ladies wore hats and gloves. You wore white gloves and shoes after Memorial Day—never before. And you wore them until Labor Day, after which you wore dark accessories.

Men wore suits and ties and hats. One of my favorite gifts for my father was to buy him a new Dobbs fedora in the form of a miniature hat, complete with tiny hatbox, which passed for a gift certificate to be redeemed for the full-size item.

Frank was two years older than Fannie. Actually, two years and two days. Their birthdays were January 10 and January 12. I too was born in January, on the eighteenth, and one of the delights of my childhood was to have my mother recount to me the story of how I was supposed to be born on the eleventh, but arrived seven days late. January 10, 11, and 12.

I used to amuse myself with that thought, wishing we had had the distinction of those consecutive birthdates.

They met at a wedding. Their mutual friends Dot and Barney Udelson got married, and Frank Manson and Fannie Franklin began their own friendship at the Udelson wedding, a friendship that would eventually lead them to the altar.

My father's bachelor days as a handsome young man-about-town and my mother's days as a young, attractive single lady were about to end. He was twenty-nine and she was twenty-seven.

XIII. The Roaring Twenties

One wife is enough for any man.

—Abraham ibn Ezra

ON JANUARY 30, 1927, Miss Bertha Gerber gave a bridge party in honor of her lifelong friend, Miss Frances Franklin on the occasion of Fannie's forthcoming May 3 marriage to Frank Manson. On April 6 at the Little Club in Roxbury, Bertha Gerber again played hostess along with Fannie's sister Bessie at a shower for the bride.

May of 1927 was an exciting time for new beginnings. On the twentieth of the month, pilot Charles Lindbergh became the first person to fly alone, non-stop, across the Atlantic Ocean. From Roosevelt Field on Long Island, the *Spirit of St. Louis* took off in the early morning hours to attempt a feat never before accomplished. With no radio and no parachute aboard the plane and with only a little compass pasted to the windshield with chewing gum, Lindbergh took his historic flight as the world held its breath and waited.

In a little over thirty-three hours, Lucky Lindy—as the press tagged him—landed at Le Bourget Airport, just outside Paris to find, to his astonishment, 100,000 people on hand to greet him. Later, in New York City, four million people turned out for a parade in his honor.

The nation went wild with excitement as a new hero—and a new age of aviation—was hailed. Just one year later, Amelia Earhart would become the first woman to fly across the Atlantic.

It was an age of "firsts." In 1927, the film industry and the nation welcomed the first "talkie" movie. Starring Al Jolson, the son of a cantor, *The Jazz Singer* became an instant hit. No more would there be silent movies. Now a clamoring public could hear their screen idols speak and sing. The revolutionary change was exciting for most, but for a film star whose voice was thin or high or just not in keeping with his screen image, the advent of "talkies" was the beginning of the end.

In 1927, Babe Ruth, the most celebrated athlete of his time, hit his record-making sixty home runs for his New York Yankees. The Babe's record held for more than thirty years until 1961, when Yankee Roger Maris hit sixty-one home runs, a record which stood until 1998 when Mark McGwire established a new and astonishing record of seventy.

Babe Ruth, besides being a pretty good ball player and one of the most popular, charismatic athletes of all time, was also a pretty good wage earner for his time. The incongruity of how we reward our super athletes and entertainers was highlighted when it was pointed out to Ruth that his salary was greater than that of the president of the United States. The Babe replied, "Well, I had a better year than he did."

Calvin Coolidge, the taciturn New Englander, was the thirtieth president, having succeeded to the office as vice president upon the death of President Warren G. Harding in 1923. Coolidge remained president until 1929, when he decided he had had enough. "I do not choose to run…" was Coolidge's famous unbattle cry, a statement typical of a man known for his curt, perfunctory remarks. Once, at a dinner party, a guest tweaked him by saying, "I've made a bet that I can get you to say more than two words to me." "You lose," replied Coolidge.

> Mr. and Mrs. William Franklin request the honor of your
> presence at the marriage of their daughter Frances to Mr.
> Frank Manson on Tuesday, the third of May, nineteen hundred
> and twenty-seven at seven o'clock, Belmont Hall, 150 Humboldt Avenue, Roxbury, Massachusetts.

They look very handsome in their wedding picture. Decked out in white tie and tails, my father stands beaming and proud. His dark hair, even then beginning to thin a bit, is slicked back in the style of the time. My mother, her soft brown hair framing her round face, is lovely in her wedding gown of lace. The hem of the gown ends in handkerchief points at mid-calf, and it is the headpiece that provides the yards of lace swirling at her feet.

My mother kept a hand-written list of the items in her trousseau and their cost. Her wedding gown is not listed, but her veil cost $7.00 and her white shoes were $4.00. Also mentioned are bridesmaids' gifts ($11.00), and a negligee ($9.00). My mother also kept a list of wedding guests, with check marks and gift items next to their names. It would seem that Dot and Barney Udelson gave curtains, while Celia and Herby Udelson gave a waffle set. So did Bea Leavitt. Rose Gerstein gave a candy jar; Bertha Gerber's gift was a lamp, and Eli Levine's present was a silver dish. Among the usual gifts of fruit bowls and vases, and candlesticks, and linens was a truly inspired gift of "bird cage and canary." The imaginative gift-giver is not named. The dollar sign next to the groom's parents' names would suggest that their wedding gift was money. The bride's parents gave the wedding.

Over one hundred people toasted the new couple, and numerous telegrams were read signaling regrets from those unable to attend. From Los Angeles came greetings from "Mr. and Mrs. Frumkin and Daughter." Miss Goldie Levinson sent her congratulations from Auburn, Maine. Mr. and Mrs. S.J. Butler from New Haven, Connecticut, sent their best wishes.

But I am partial to the telegram from the "First National Sandwich Shop, Inc." of Boston: "A barrell [sic] of blessings, best wishes and joy and in a year maybe a boy." My mother's favorite luncheon place near the State House made up in good intentions what they lacked in prescience. Fannie and Frank would wait seven years for me, their only child.

If the 1920s were known as the Jazz Age, it was with good reason. That decade saw the rise of that singularly American music born in the South and raised in Chicago. It was nurtured by black musicians, and its strong, syncopated rhythms captivated the country, particularly the young, the "Flaming Youth" of the '20s.

Louis Armstrong, Bessy Smith, Duke Ellington, all were part of the exciting, explosive new music. It wasn't classical music; it wasn't Broadway show tunes or even the popular Tin Pan Alley songs of the day. But it had elements of them all, and then some stuff that was purely its own. How else could you explain it? "What's jazz?" exclaimed musician Fats Waller. "If you don't know, I can't tell you."

People went to the movies, as many as ninety million a week to see their screen heroes, Charlie Chaplin, Rudolph Valentino, Clara Bow, and Greta Garbo. And radio, the fledgling entertainment medium that came right into your own living room, was capturing a national audience. In 1922, only 60,000 American families owned radios; by 1930, that figure had risen to almost fourteen million.*

At the beginning of the decade, women's skirt lengths were six or seven inches above the ground. By 1927, they had risen to knee-height. One theory has it that women's hemlines are an accurate barometer of economic times. The longer the skirt, the tougher the times; the shorter, the better the economy. Throughout the decade of the twenties, the skirts

---

This Fabulous Century, Vol. III. p. 101.

kept getting shorter.

Yes, in 1927, things were good. Nothing much had changed since ancient Rome, when Juvenal said, "Two things only the people anxiously desire—bread and circuses." Bread seemed plentiful as the economy prospered. And the "circus" in the form of movies, radio, and fads such as the game of Mah Jong and tabloid scandals offered entertainment for the masses.

The automobile gave people more mobility than ever before. Gas stations, garages, hotels, and restaurants "on the road" grew enormously to service a car-happy public. On December 2, 1927, when Henry Ford brought out the Model A, "one million people tried to get into the Ford headquarters in New York to catch a glimpse of it."* All over the country, that scene was repeated; such was America's love affair with the automobile, a romance that to this day shows no sign of abating.

Prosperity. People were buying more and spending more. "Between 1922 and 1927, the purchasing power of American wages increased at the rate of more than two per cent annually."* Americans were also speculating more in the stock market. The boom gave every indication of going on forever.

And there was Prohibition. The Eighteenth Amendment to the Constitution went into effect in January of 1920, prohibiting the "manufacture, sale, or transportation of intoxicating liquors." The conventional wisdom of the time was that the evils of liquor had been amply demonstrated and that Americans were more than ready to accept a "dry" country.

That was not, however, to be the case. Very quickly, the law was perceived as foolish, unworkable, and wrong. Resourceful and illegal ways were found to circumvent the law, spawning some ingenious methods as well as adding some colorful phrases to the national lexicon: "bathtub gin," "bootleggers," and "speakeasies." They all hinted at the new lawless atmosphere surrounding drinking in the twenties.

Bathtub gin referred to the concoction of pseudo gin that was mixed up in a vat or, in some cases, a bathtub. "Bootleggers" was the swashbuckling term applied to those criminals who were bringing rum and other whiskey in from abroad—the illicit cargo being transferred from ships in the harbor to fast cabin cruisers to trucks and then delivered to speakeasies, which were underground drinking clubs where you could "speak easy," uttering the magic password that gained you entry.

The whole country seemed to be in revolt. And having a rip-roaring good time of it too.

---

*Allen Frederick Lewis. *Only Yesterday*. p. 135.
Ibid. p. 139.

XIV. Depression

As long as a person breathes, he should not lose hope.

—The Talmud

"WHY," I USED TO ASK MY MOTHER in my most accusatory tone, "why didn't you have any more children? Why couldn't I have had brothers or sisters?" Her regretful, patient response was always the same: The Depression.

As a kid, I am sure I didn't know—and certainly didn't understand—what the Depression had to do with the size of my family, even though my mother tried to convey to me how anxious and worrisome a time that was. My father was out of work, and there wasn't much money. There was even less hope. It would have been reckless and irresponsible to have more babies. In fact, the birth rate showed a decided downturn during those years, falling from 18.9 per thousand population in 1929 to 16.5 in 1933.*

Historians trace the beginning of the Depression to October 29, 1929. But that was in retrospect; on that terrible day there may have been a lot of name-calling, but it would have been premature for anyone to have the historical vision to know what hard times lay ahead. All anyone knew was that a sense of panic had overtaken the country as the stock market crashed on that fateful day, a day that came to be known as Black Tuesday.

With the stock market crash, millions of investors lost their money. Stock losses for 1929–31 were estimated at $50 billion. Businesses went into bankruptcy, and unemployment rose so that by 1923 twelve million

*Allen, Frederick Lewis. *Since Yesterday*. p. 107.

Americans were out of work. A worldwide depression had set in, the worst in Western history.

Soup kitchens did a brisk business feeding the impoverished. People without money or food stood in bread lines for the meager rations that were doled out. Before the Depression, anyone earning over $5,000 was considered well-to-do. During the early years of the Depression, an average doctor made about $3,300, a secretary earned about $1,000, and a public school teacher made $1,227.*

During the years of 1932 to 1934, a man's wool suit cost $10.50; a new Chrysler sedan sold for $995. Milk was ten cents a quart, and it would cost you twenty-nine cents for a pound of sirloin steak.

And Frank Manson was out of work. My mother went back to work at the State House, to her former job as secretary-stenographer. She was making about $1,000 a year. Prior to the Depression, married ladies who worked were frowned upon. The husband carried the status—and the burden—of being the breadwinner. A working wife suggested that a husband just couldn't cut it.

But during the Depression all that changed. Everyone worked, as everyone was in the same boat. And a decidedly leaky boat it was at that. You didn't spend much time worrying about status when you had to plug up the leaks. All anybody was concerned about was earning enough money to put bread on the table.

In my mother's case, it would seem that she was not all that unhappy to be going back to work, to a job she loved. At the State House she enjoyed the satisfaction and pride of doing a job of which she was extremely capable. She delighted in the companionship of her colleagues, the camaraderie of the office and, of course, in earning a much-needed salary.

My dad, always eager and energetic, took whatever work he could find. It could not have been too hard, since he liked people and they liked him. He could tell jokes, talk sports, play bridge and poker. He could win without gloating and lose without whining. When finally he was hired as an appliance salesman by Jordan Marsh Company, New England's largest department store, he was relieved to be back on a payroll.

The winter of 1934 was unusually cold. "The Atlantic Ocean was blocked with ice all the way from Nantucket Island to the mainland."†
On January 18, I was born at the Faulkner Hospital in Jamaica Plain,

---

*This Fabulous Century, Vol. III . p. 24.
†Allen, Frederick Lewis. Since Yesterday. p. 138

weighing in at seven pounds, seven ounces. As was the custom of the day, my mother stayed in the hospital, "lying-in" for two weeks.

In 1934, President Franklin Delano Roosevelt was in the second year of his first term, having been elected by an anxious citizenry that was fearful of what the future held. Could this strong, confident, patrician Easterner help? Would he have some answers?

Roosevelt's first inaugural address sent a message the country was eager to hear. "This great nation will endure as it has endured, will revive and will prosper. So, first of all, let me assert my firm belief that the only thing we have to fear is fear itself."

Roosevelt set a standard in his first one hundred days of unprecedented and bold activism. The White House pushed for all manner of social and economic reform. And Congress went along, falling under the spell of the master politician newly ensconced in the Oval Office.

The New Deal was off and running. An alphabet soup of programs was enacted, programs designed to save and protect workers, farmers, consumers. There was the WPA, NRA, PWA, CCC, SEC and TVA. The latter, the Tennessee Valley Authority, built dams and brought electricity to that impoverished part of the country. The WPA, the Works Progress Administration, was based on the premise of finding work for the millions of unemployed Americans.

The CCC, the Civilian Conservation Corps, put men to work in the country's forests; the PWA, the Public Works Administration, put people to work on the nation's bridges, roads, and public buildings. The Security Exchange Commission was created to oversee and regulate the stock market. And, after fourteen years, Prohibition came to an end, repealed by the twenty-first amendment to the Constitution.

While my birth certainly was a notable event for my family in 1934, the birth of five other little girls that year attracted a good deal more attention. On May 28, Mrs. Oliva Dionne of Callender, Ontario, gave birth to quintuplets. Emelie, Yvonne, Marie, Annette, and Cecile were instant celebrities, exciting world attention. Unfortunately that attention was exploited, and the quints were turned into commercial properties throughout their early years. By most accounts, their lives were not happy.

No such fate awaited me. My mother's conscientious notes about her baby indicate that my worst problem was that I "spit up orange juice." But I must have been something of a worry for my mother, as most babies were to over-anxious, first-time parents in those pre-Doctor Spock days of more rigid child-rearing.

At two months, my mother noted that I weighed eleven pounds, four ounces, which caused her to scribble, "Is she getting enough?" Mother's notebook detailing my diet and care as an infant sounds anything but relaxing. The cream of wheat cereal had to be "cooked three hours." Starting me on eggs at six months of age meant giving me a quarter of an egg for two or three days before increasing my portion to a half then to a whole egg. There must have been times when my mother wondered if she was more a chemist than a mother, what with all the measuring and mixing she was undertaking.

Throughout the summer of 1934, my mother kept mixing and measuring and I kept growing and thriving. But as the winter had been an unusually cold one, so was the summer especially hot. Particularly in the midwest, where in Kansas the temperature stayed at 108 degrees or above for weeks. Farmers already suffering the economic woes of the Depression were now handed another cruel blow by nature.

Along with drought and winds, dust storms swept through the area, reducing the good earth to sand. John Steinbeck's *The Grapes of Wrath*, generally regarded as one of the best American novels of the twentieth century, tells the powerful and devastating story of these victims of the Dust Bowl.

That summer the nation's attention was briefly captured by a real-life gangster saga. Public Enemy number one, John Dillinger, was gunned down on a Chicago street as he came out of a movie theater, ending a career in crime yet spawning an enduring legend, to say nothing of forthcoming books and movies.

In 1935, under Roosevelt, the Social Security Act was established, creating a system of insurance and benefits for unemployed and disabled workers as well as retirees.

In Europe, the forces of fascism were rumbling through the continent, particularly in Germany, Italy, and Spain. But Americans were otherwise occupied as the Depression wore on. And my mother got her handwriting analyzed by "Jeanne French, Internationally Famous Graphologist," from Cleveland, Ohio.

"Prominent among your traits is a serious sense of responsibility and honor, which gives balance and stability to your character. You are dependable, optimistic and mildly dignified.... You are loyal...and sincere.... There is nothing flighty or capricious in your nature.... You get much pleasure out of friends and social life and probably can boast of friendships of long standing. The theater and amusements hold some charm for you.... You enjoy music and good books...." This analysis is unerringly correct.

As always, people took time out from their workaday lives and worries for amusement and novelty. The movies were tremendously popular, as something like eighty-five million Americans plunked down their twenty-five cents every week to go to the cinema. Disney's first full-length animated feature, *Snow White*, was an instant hit; so was *The Wizard of Oz* with Judy Garland.

The gods and goddesses of the silver screen who captivated audiences were Clark Gable, Bette Davis, Jimmy Stewart, Humphrey Bogart, Joan Crawford, and Gary Cooper. Gangster films featuring Jimmy Cagney or Edward G. Robinson were popular. The Marx Brothers and W.C. Fields starred in the comedies. Child star Shirley Temple earned a special place in the hearts of Americans, and Fred Astaire and Ginger Rogers epitomized gaiety and grace as they danced their way into celluloid history.

But the most dramatic story of 1936 was not on any screen. It was being played out in London's Buckingham Palace, where the King of England, Edward VIII, was in love. However, the object of his affection was deemed by royal standards as well as by the British public to be highly inappropriate. The lady was, after all, an American.

As if being American were not bad enough, there was yet another problem, even more insurmountable. She was divorced. Wallis Warfield Simpson was a charmer from Baltimore, and Britain's king was smitten. But British law would allow him to marry neither a divorcee nor an American. And so on December 11, 1936, as the world listened, the king made the following public announcement: "I have found it impossible to carry the heavy burden of responsibility and to discharge my duties as king as I should wish to do, without the help of the woman I love."

This abdication speech, forever after referred to as the "Woman I Love" speech, set the stage for Edward's brother George to assume the throne. Edward and Wallis were married in 1937, becoming the Duke and Duchess of Windsor. They lived a life of luxury, traveling in high society and "enjoying" what many observers characterized as the life of the idle rich.

George VI was beloved by his people, and ruled until his death in 1952, whereupon his daughter, Elizabeth, the present queen, succeeded him as Great Britain's monarch.

In 1936, civil war broke out in Spain. The forces of fascist Generalissimo Francisco Franco fought against the leftist loyalist troops. The cause of freedom championed by the loyalists ignited sympathizers throughout the world. More than 3,000 American men, spurred by idealism, socialism, and visions of liberty went to Spain to fight in a volunteer unit called the Abraham Lincoln Brigade. My cousin, Burton Manson, Ned's son, was one of them. By the time the war ended with

Franco's victory in 1939, more than one million people had lost their lives. Burton Manson was one of them.

In 1936, on January 10, my mother's thirty-sixth birthday, her father, William Franklin, died at the age of seventy-eight. His wife, Jennie, his ten children, their spouses and children survived him. Only a two-year-old, I kept no memories of my grandfather, but the photographs of him, young and old, show a handsome man with a full head of thick hair, first brown, then snow-white. He had a full mustache, and his face, with its firm, square jaw, conveyed both strength and kindness.

When my mother went back to work at her job at the State House, I went to daycare. But not just any daycare; I went to the Hecht House. Originally called the Hebrew Industrial School in the 1890s, it later became the Hecht Neighborhood House. Named for Jacob and Lina Hecht, prominent Boston Jewish citizens who had helped establish community services for nineteenth-century Jewish immigrants, it offered recreational and cultural programs and, starting in the 1920s, the first Jewish nursery school in Boston.

In 1936, the Hecht House moved out of the West End and into the old quarters of the Home for Jewish Children at 160 American Legion Highway in Dorchester. There I played in the sandbox, ran and fell and skinned my knees—which seems to have been an event of some regularity, since early childhood photos always show me with scraped knees or sporting a Band-Aid.

It was at the Hecht House that I sang "The Farmer in the Dell" and refused to take the required midday nap. I can still see the line of cots, a seemingly endless row of beds with identical army-issue khaki blankets. Among that parade of sleeping preschoolers, only I seemed unable, or unwilling, to close my eyes. Usually the most cooperative of children, regularly gaining teachers' approval, I found that my slumber habits earned me demerits, causing my teachers to mention this stubborn sleeper syndrome to my mother.

In 1937, as Americans continued to struggle with the effects of the Depression, President Roosevelt began a second term. His inaugural address acknowledged the difficulties he and the country still faced: "I see one third of a nation ill-housed, ill-clad, ill-nourished."

Roosevelt's popularity was still enormous. The country's most beloved entertainer, cowboy-comedian-philosopher Will Rogers, commented, "America hasn't been happy in three years as [it] is today, no money, no banks, no work, no nothing, but they know they got a man in there who is wise to Congress, wise to our so-called big men. The whole country is with him, just so he does something. If he burned down the

Capitol, we would cheer and say, 'well, we at least got a fire started anyhow.'"

My memories of the 1930s are, of course, limited. But I do recall the day when the world seemed to be coming to an end. I was four-and-a-half on September 21, 1938, when a hurricane hit New England with devastating effect and without any warning, taking 700 lives as it roared up the east coast.

I was with a babysitter, and I can't recall her name or what she looked like. I only remember her housedress of tiny flowers. I remember that because I was sitting on her lap and I could almost feel those flowers. How sweet and nice they were, the way things were supposed to be, rather than the way they were outside our third-floor apartment window, where the world was coming apart.

I didn't cry. I must have worried about my parents' safety, but my strongest memory is one of awe. I'd never seen anything like this storm, of course; few people had. The raging weather taking place beyond the window, beyond the glass, was a little like the fascination of a snow globe. Shake it up and magic happens. Only a snow globe was gentle and make-believe; what was happening outside was violent and terribly real.

Sturdy oaks and elms swayed and snapped and crashed to the ground. Torrents of rain fell from the blackened sky. The howling wind seemed to fill my ears and the apartment until it was the only sound I heard. I don't recall when or how my parents made their way home, only that they did. And after that, the storm held more fascination than fright for me.

Among my other very early memories of that time were my first visits to New York City to visit my mother's sister Betty. At that time there was an overnight boat from Boston to New York, and I was going on it. Taking the Boat Train with my mother, sharing a cabin that held upper and lower berths, filled me with delight.

I remember my first taxi ride and the excitement I felt. I was so thrilled that I couldn't sit down, and as we careered through the streets of Manhattan my mother warned me that I would get hurt if I didn't sit down. Well, I didn't [sit], and I did [get hurt]. But one cut lip, an omen of all the subsequent dangers that would afflict New York, has not dissuaded me. I'll take Manhattan. Still.

In the summer of 1939, when I was five, we went again to New York, to the World's Fair. During its two-year run, forty-five million people would visit the exposition, whose theme was "The World of Tomorrow." Its exhibits and pavilions were dedicated to showing how technology would transform the world into something streamlined, efficient and miraculous.

It was there that I saw television for the first time and marveled at the moving pictures in the magic box. It was said that someday everyone would have one in his home. Surely that was fantasy. But it was a fantasy that would become reality in less than a decade.

The "World of Tomorrow," however, was taking a distinct back seat to the headlines of the day. For 1939 was also the year that Hitler's German army marched into Poland, signaling the start of war in Europe. And in that fateful year, on the eve of the Holocaust, there were seven million Jews living in Europe, of whom only one million would survive.

On September 3, 1939, the weary and defeated British Prime Minister Neville Chamberlain, read this statement: "This morning the British Ambassador in Berlin handed to the German government a final note stating that unless we heard from them by eleven o'clock that they were preparing at once to withdraw their troops from Poland, a state of war would exist between us. I have to tell you that no such undertaking has been received, and in consequence this country is at war with Germany."

XV. America Goes to War

I have said this before but I shall say it again and again.
Your boys are not going to be sent into any foreign wars.

—*President Franklin D. Roosevelt*
October 30, 1940 at Boston Garden

ON JULY 5, 1941, IN DAVID-GORODOK, the village next to Korzan-gorodok, the Germans ordered all male Jews over the age of fourteen to gather by the church. They were herded together and taken outside of town. There they were forced to dig trenches, trenches that became their own graves when they were shot, murdered by the Nazi SS troops.

In 1941, there were 134 million people in the United States. The median income was around $2,000 a year and good men's suits could be had for $35 to $40. Even as war raged in Europe, Americans were still hoping that the United States could stay out of the war, although that hope was diminishing. And in a 1941 Gallup poll, Americans were asked which was more important: that we stay out of the war, or that Germany be defeated. Sixty-eight percent of the respondents replied that it was more important to defeat Germany.

Sunday afternoon, December 7, 1941. It was cozy and snug in our third-floor apartment at 1390 Beacon Street in Brookline. Like most Americans in pretelevision America, my mother, father, and I were having a quiet day at home in front of the radio. In warmer weather we might have gone out for a Sunday drive—people did that then—but it was winter now, and we were at home.

I was lying on the living room floor reading the "funnies," the Sunday newspaper comics section. My father would have been reading the paper; so would my mother. Or she might be at the bridge table working one of the beautiful wooden jigsaw puzzles that she often rented from the lending library.

That morning we would have had our usual Sunday breakfast of bacon and eggs, and my mother would have argued with me about drinking my milk. "It's good for you. It helps your bones get strong. How do you expect to grow if you don't drink your milk?" I hated milk.

Just weeks short of my eighth birthday, I was happily looking forward to that milestone even as I engaged in my annual debate with my parents concerning the upcoming Christmas holiday.

"Why can't we have a tree?" I pleaded. "They're so pretty, please, please, please...." The answer was simple, swift, and always the same: No. We are Jewish. It was the identical plea I would hear years later from my own daughter, followed by the same reply.

At a few minutes after three that afternoon of December 7, the radio suddenly barked out an announcement. My parents stiffened, the newspaper falling from my father's hands to the floor as we heard, "We interrupt this program to bring you a special news bulletin. The Japanese have attacked Pearl Harbor."

What did it mean? Where was Pearl Harbor, anyway? Was this war? We were stunned and anxious. As in any crisis facing our family, my mother got on the phone and called her sisters. No one knew anything. We were all to learn together, very quickly, that we were indeed at war.

The next day President Franklin Roosevelt went before a joint session of Congress and delivered this statement: "Yesterday, December 7, 1941, a date which will live in infamy, the United States was suddenly and deliberately attacked by naval and air forces of the empire of Japan. I ask that Congress declare that since the unprovoked and dastardly attack by Japan...a state of war has existed between the United States and the Japanese Empire."

With the vote of every United States Senator and every member of the House of Representatives save one—pacifist Jeannette Rankin—the president got his support. Three days later Germany and Italy declared war on the United States and, as my father put it, "we're in it now." We were at war in Europe and in the Pacific.

To my generation, the bombing of Pearl Harbor, our naval base in Hawaii, came to be one of those events in our lives that carried a permanent emotional imprint. Like the terrible November day when John F. Kennedy was assassinated, December 7, 1941, was a day we would always remember. We would forever after be able to recall where we were and what we were doing when we heard the news.

Sixteen million men and women would serve in America's armed forces in World War II. Two hundred and seventy-four thousand would lose their lives in battle. One of them was my cousin Harold Barton, Betty's son. A navy pilot stationed in England with Joseph P. Kennedy, Jr., Harold was thirty-one years old when he was killed over the Atlantic in 1944.

We were at war on two fronts: in the Pacific and in Europe. While the "boys" were overseas, life on the home front was for the most part confident and committed to the war effort. Women in unprecedented numbers went to work in the shipyards and offices and on the production lines, freeing men for combat. Army and navy recruiting offices were swamped with people wanting to enlist. By June 1942, "more than seven million people were involved in the ranks of America's civil defense."[*] My father was one of them; he was an air-raid warden.

Wardens were given armbands, helmets, and whistles along with assignments to patrol their city blocks or neighborhoods. My dad was proud of his contribution and took his duties seriously. When the siren sounded indicating an air-raid drill, he would take his post on the roof of our apartment building, scanning the sky for enemy planes as well as surveying the neighborhood for any violations of the "lights out" requirement.

Streetlights and neon signs went off; people pulled down their "black-out" window shades, and in minutes the city went dark. It was eerie and it was exciting. All of this was practice for the time when enemy bombers might one night fly overhead. If that time should ever come—which it never did—we were going to make very sure that there were no visible targets.

As the lights went out at home, they went out elsewhere. Indeed, one of the many patriotic wartime songs brought hope and tears with its sentiment of "when the lights go on again all over the world...." Paris, the City of Light, was dark and occupied by the Nazis. Unlike American cities, London had been experiencing the real thing in nighttime bombings. The German *Blitz* meant that night after night Nazi planes flew over Britain dropping their bombs, bringing destruction and death, but never destroying the spirit of the English people.

The queen of England, King George's wife, exemplified that resolve when she was asked why she didn't leave London, or at least send her little daughters, Princess Elizabeth and Princess Margaret away to the country, to safety. "The children will not leave me; I will never leave the king," Queen Elizabeth said, "and the king will never leave London." Not

*Lingeman, Richard R. *Don't You Know There's A War On?* p. 62.

even when the bombs fell on Buckingham palace.

It was a time when patriotism became more than the words of a song or the echoing of a slogan. We *believed* that we, the Allies—America, Britain, France, and Russia—would prevail. And toward that end we tried to do what we could. My mother knitted sweaters and scarves for the soldiers overseas. My father tried to enlist, but while the sentiment was laudable, the reality of a forty-three-year-old married father was not acceptable to the military. My dad had to settle for regular trips to the blood bank to donate blood. My mother rolled bandages at the Red Cross center. So did I. And she wrote letters overseas through a pen pal organization whose purpose was to see that every soldier far from home got mail.

Even I wrote. They were little letters penned by a nine- or ten-year-old girl intended to cheer a war-weary soldier. My cousins Stanley and Earl Franklin, Charlie's sons, were both in the service. Earl was sent to the Pacific to Okinawa, and Stanley was in Europe. I wrote to Stanley, and he actually wrote back to me. Waiting for the mail became a major occupation—and preoccupation—of the war. Millions of letters were sent to servicemen, and millions were written in reply, "so many, in fact, that to save shipping space the War Department devised a miniaturized letter form known as V-mail."[*] V, of course, stood for Victory.

Every line of every letter was read by a censor and receiving mail with words or phrases, even whole sentences, blacked out was not uncommon. I saved those letters from Cousin Stanley for the longest time. I wish I had them still.

At school we bought War Stamps to be used toward the purchase of War Bonds or Savings Bonds. My Girl Scout troop collected tin cans and newspapers, which were turned in at collection points around the city. I had trouble visualizing, at my age, how those items were reused for the war effort. Would soldiers possibly want to read old funny papers? Really? And if you squashed up tin cans, what did they do with them afterwards?

Newspapers could be recycled and used for the packaging of weapons being shipped overseas. The scrap-metal drives all over the country yielded huge amounts of material to be recycled into weapons. In contradiction to the old biblical imperative to "turn one's weapons into ploughshares," Americans by the millions were doing just the opposite. The iron, for example, in one old shovel would make four hand grenades.

Americans faced their wartime duties with patriotic zeal. Practically

---

[*]Baily, Ronald H. *The Home Front: USA.* p. 108.

every family had someone away in the service, "fighting for our country." You would see the telltale banners hanging in windows; a single star against a white field, the star representing a son or brother or husband in the service. Sometimes there would be more than one star. And sometimes there would be a gold star. More than a badge of honor, the gold star was a tragic sign of loss. It represented a loved one who had died in service to his country.

Everyone knew someone in the war. If it wasn't an immediate relative, it was a cousin, a neighbor, or your best friend's brother. My cousins Lester Franklin along with Stanley and Earl Franklin were "in it." Cousin Harold Barton was a casualty of the war. No wonder people at home felt that they should do whatever they could to help.

Victory gardens were a case in point. They popped up everywhere, in empty city lots, tiny backyard plots, anywhere where people could grow their own fruits and vegetables. There would be nearly twenty million victory gardens before the war was over. Rationing began in 1942. Based on a complicated system of ration books and stamps, each man, woman, and child in the country was allotted a certain number of points with which to purchase hard-to-get items. For example, each person was allowed forty-eight blue points, to be redeemed for canned goods, and sixty-four red points, to be used for the purchase of meats and dairy products. So, for my family of three my mother had a total of 144 blue points and 192 red points each month to shop for our food needs. (In 1943, hamburger patties sold for forty-three cents a pound and required eight points per pound.)

Sugar was rationed, and therefore my mother didn't bake as much as she used to. And maybe my father couldn't have his coffee as sweet as he liked. But for hard-core coffee drinkers, sugar was the least of their problems. Coffee was also rationed: one cup of java a day was it. Sunday drives became a thing of the past, since rubber and gasoline were severely rationed. If you couldn't get tires for your car, and if the average driver, like my dad, was only allotted three to five gallons of gas a week, then family outings in the country became sweet memories for most Americans.

There were complaints about the home front deprivations, from those who found the restrictions of rationing onerous. There were those who found their way around rationing and who trafficked in the black market where you could buy whatever you wanted for a price. Some indulged in hoarding, in buying up and stocking goods. But most people followed the rules and scorned those who did not. The rallying cry of the faithful was "Don't you know there's a war on?" a phrase that identified

559167 EP

WAR RATION BOOK No. 3

Void if altered

O.P.A.
VALID
U S A
VALID

Address and Sign
**WITHOUT
STAMP**

Identification of person to whom issued: PRINT IN FULL

Natalie L. Manson

(First name)   (Middle name)   (Last name)

Street number or rural route   1390 Beacon St.

City or post office   Brookline   State   Mass.

AGE	SEX	WEIGHT	HEIGHT	OCCUPATION
9	F	82 Lbs.	Ft. In.	School

SIGNATURE   Natalie L. Manson

(Person to whom book is issued. If such person is unable to sign because of age or incapacity, another may sign in his behalf.)

LOCAL BOARD ACTION

Issued by ....

(Local board number)   (Date)

Street address ....

City ....   State ....

(Signature of issuing officer)

BOOK 4 ISSUED

not only the need for sacrifice but the unity of purpose for Americans on the home front.

Indeed, publicity—or propaganda, if you will—in the form of slogans, movies, and songs, all sought to remind the American public that it had a job to do as well. And to most people, life at home, altered and deprived as it was—seemed more than bearable compared to the fighting our "boys" were enduring. Not to be outdone or overlooked, the "girls" were "in this thing" too. All of the armed forces had their women's divisions, established so that women could perform non-combat duties, thus freeing up the men for combat.

In the Army, the WACS (Women's Army Corps) served as technicians, nurses, secretaries, and clerks. Over 100,000 women joined the WACS. The WAVES performed similar duties in the navy as did the WAAFS in the Army Air Corps and the SPARS in the Coast Guard.

At home we monitored and followed the war as it progressed overseas. Or, as was the case in the early days of the war, through a lack of progress. The eventual outcome was never in doubt; America had never lost a war; we would prevail. But still there were terrible losses of men and battles. We read the news stories, avidly followed the newsreels in the theaters, and read *Life* magazine every week. Hollywood went to war as stars like Jimmy Stewart and Clark Gable enlisted. Bob Hope was off entertaining the troops in battle zones, and at home the Hollywood Canteen became a symbol of dedication to the war effort.

The Hollywood Canteen was like all USO (United Service Organizations) canteens around the country, and at the same time it was totally unique. Yes, it was a haven, a place where a weary G.I. could get free food, hear some music, and relax. But only in Hollywood might a soldier get a chance to dance with a movie queen like Hedy Lamarr or be served dinner by Jimmy Cagney. If the elite of Hollywood could do regular chores, why so could everyone else.

America's popular music echoes the anxious yearnings of the people. When Bing Crosby crooned "White Christmas," the images of servicemen around the world being away from home for the holidays created heartache and hope. When The Andrews Sisters sang "Don't Sit Under the Apple Tree (with Anyone Else But Me)" the lilting air of the tune highlighted the plight of lovers who were separated and who dreamed of being reunited. When that day would come, nobody knew.

XVI. The Home Front

Use it up, wear it out, make it do or do without.

—*Wartime motto*

BEFORE LATTERDAY TWENTIETH-CENTURY Americans "invented" recycling, World War II Americans were doing it. Women saved old nylon stockings, since "23,000 pairs went into making one parachute."* Housewives saved kitchen fat. I remember my mother pouring the hot bacon grease from her skillet into a tin can. When it cooled, hardened, and the can was filled up, she turned it in at the local center. One pound of fat contained enough glycerin to make a pound of black powder, or enough for fifty .30-caliber bullets.†

We saved our old clothes, which were packed up and shipped out as Bundles for Britain. England was suffering the ravages of war, and the shortage of goods was well beyond what we Americans experienced. Despite the war, life on the home front continued pretty much unabated. Americans still liked to be entertained, and my family was no exception. At night we gathered around the radio to listen to the shows that America loved.

Kate Smith singing *God Bless America* became an icon to the listening public; but the best fun, of course, was the comedians: Jack Benny, Bob Hope, Edgar Bergen and Charlie McCarthy. It never occurred to me (nor, apparently, to anyone else) that there might be something slightly odd in featuring a ventriloquist and his wooden dummy on the *radio*. We

---

*Lingeman, Richard. *Don't You Know There's A War On?* p. 248.
†*Ibid.*

all just blithely visualized Charlie as a personality of his own and, who knew—or cared—whether Edgar Bergen moved his lips or not. Despite the violent upheaval of war, it surely was a more innocent time.

In school we children did what kids always do, whether it's war or peace. We giggled and played; we tried to be quiet and behave for our teachers; we knew it was our duty to hate substitute teachers; and we worried about whether everybody would like us.

We cut snowflakes out of white paper at Christmastime and pasted them on the windows; we made pink hearts at Valentine's Day and waited impatiently at our desks while the "postman" (the teacher's designated student) delivered our cards to us. We filed into the school auditorium for holiday "assemblies" and watched plays, pageants, and "educational movies," but never without the film projector breaking down.

In the classroom, each desk had an inkwell built into it, and standard equipment for every schoolchild included pencils and pens, real pens, the kind you dipped in the shiny black liquid and had to wipe off on the side of the well. Too little ink and you were scratching out words that couldn't be seen; too much ink and it dribbled all over your work papers.

We didn't have much of a library at home, but my mother was nevertheless a reader. She was forever taking books out of the lending library, a bookstore where, for a small fee, you could rent the latest best-seller. There were no paperback books. My mother would take out Ellery Queen mysteries for my father who devoured them. I read Nancy Drew mysteries and anything else I could get my hands on. The other books I loved were coloring books. The smell and feel of a smooth crayon was somehow a joy. I wonder how many other children flirted with the idea of becoming an artist just because of early encounters with Crayolas.

As dreamy and hopeful as I may have been, I still had a fairly sober side to my nature. I was, after all, my mother's daughter. For example, I had a doll named Ruthie. I adored her, but I grew to dislike her name. "Change it," my mother surprisingly advised. But I knew I couldn't do that. Somehow I knew about rules and consequences; I'd made a mistake in naming her, it's true; well, I was going to have to live with it. Or more accurately, Ruthie was going to have to live with it and be Ruthie to the end of her days.

Our Brookline home was an apartment on the top floor of 1390 Beacon Street. It was large, with three bedrooms, dining room, living room and a nice white tile bathroom, where I often practiced my tap dancing. I liked how the taps sounded on tile, and since my mother didn't want me scratching up her wooden floors in the other rooms, we were both happy. The Katherine Paige School of Dance, where I was enrolled, was also on Beacon Street, just a few blocks from us.

I started in second grade at the Edward Devotion School. Years later the mention of the school's name might elicit surprise. What kind of a Jewish child went to a religious school. Of course, it was nothing of the sort. The school was named for one of the town's first Yankee citizens, who died in 1744. In his will Edward Devotion left a donation to the town for the purpose of "building and maintaining a school as near the center of the said town as shall be agreed upon by the town." Apparently it took the town a while to come to that agreement. It wasn't until 1891 that the town built the school. It opened in 1894.

I found a lot to like in school, but that did not include math or gym. I certainly didn't like having to climb a rope or vault over the leather "horse." The gym uniforms we were required to wear were also terrible, I thought. Surely there were better things one could be doing. Softball and basketball were better. My major lifetime achievement in the field of athletics occurred during one memorable gym period when I heaved the basketball from the opposite end of the gym and watched in amazement as it swished through the net.

Our principal, Mr. Charles Taylor, was a kindly white-haired man whose Santa Claus eyes sparkled behind his rimless glasses. I thought he probably had come with the school. I later found out I was very nearly right. He served from 1906 to 1948.

I can still remember—it was either seventh or eighth grade—when Bobby Wool and I made an appointment—yes, an *appointment*—to see Mr. Taylor about some urgent student reform issue. I have no recollection whatsoever as to the nature of our "pressing" business, but I will always recall our appearance in his office, our sense of mission, our nervousness at being in the great man's presence and the attention, respect, and courtesy he showed us.

Reading the comics was a favorite pastime; I especially like the pretty, wide-eyed "Fritzie Ritz," featuring Nancy and Sluggo. I loved going to the movies, and I had my favorites there too, like Abbott and Costello, but definitely not the Three Stooges. Technicolor musicals were the best; anything with Fred Astaire, Gene Kelly, or Dan Dailey assured me of a perfect Saturday afternoon at the movies. Usually there was a double-feature on the bill and I liked those "Boston Blackie" crime movies in glorious black and white.

I thought it was great when my older cousin Doris Kraft took me to the Coolidge Corner Theatre for a Saturday movie. I didn't think it was so great the day she took me to see *The Phantom of the Opera* with Claude Rains. I was so terrified by the Phantom's acid-ruined face revealed under his mask that she had to take me home before the movie ended. I'm not quite sure she's forgiven me yet.

Back then you could shop at the five-and-ten cent store and actually buy things for five or ten cents. School pencils and notebooks, crayons and paper, even little vials of perfume as gifts for your mother, they were all affordable at the Coolidge Corner Woolworth's. An ice cream cone at Brigham's cost fifteen cents. We'd get an ice cream after the movies at Coolidge Corner. But if we went to the Capitol Theatre on Commonwealth Avenue, we would stop in at the deli next door. You could reach into the wooden barrel and pick out your own pickle. Half-sours, and dills, all floating in pungent and tantalizing brine; yours for a nickel.

In the winter, people who had coal stoves tossed the cooled ashes on the icy sidewalks to make them less slippery. Milkmen delivered milk and cream to your door—in glass bottles. Doctors made housecalls. So, the night when I split my right eyebrow open hitting my head on the bedpost while doing somersaults in bed, my parents' frantic call to Dr. Barney brought him post-haste.

Barney Udelson, my parents' best friend, was our faithful family physician and tended to my bouts of measles, mumps, and chicken pox. Over the phone he calmly told my mother to pinch and hold the bleeding wound together until he could get to the house. My mother not so calmly but valiantly did as instructed until Dr. Barney came, whereupon he stretched me out on the dining room table and sewed me up. The wound required three stitches.

After the shock and fear of my experience wore off, I began to view it as an opportunity. I had never broken a limb or had my tonsils or appendix out, had never been to the hospital by the ripe old age of eleven. I was determined to make the most of this injury. My mother thought I should stay home and rest after my ordeal. I insisted that I was fine. Aware of the dramatic possibilities inherent in the situation, I found Mrs. Mellus's sixth-grade class the next morning a proper forum for my little "star turn" as I repeated the story over and over each time someone asked, "What happened to *you?*"

Usually I would have been more amenable to a day off from school, whether it was due to a cold or the ubiquitous "upset stomach." At home my mother would make me comfortable in bed, fluffing up my pillows, bringing me a glass of water or ginger ale with a bendable straw, accompanied by Campbell's tomato soup with Ritz crackers for lunch. It was just about the finest thing ever; before the phrase "comfort food" was ever coined, I knew what it was.

But sick days were mostly characterized by the radio soap operas.

Our Gal Sunday was my mother's favorite, and so it was mine. It was the program that asked the question, "Can this girl from a mining town in the West find happiness as the wife of a wealthy and titled Englishman?" Fortunately for the listening audience, that longed-for state of contentment was never even a remote possibility.

Most of my friends lived in apartments, as I did. Bobby lived on Green Street at Coolidge Corner, Karla lived in a rabbit-warren first-floor apartment on Williams Street, two blocks from me, close enough so that in the spring our parents let us go out after supper for rides on our bikes.

Karla Lothrop, the eldest of three children of Reverend Donald and Helena Lothrop, was a blond, laughing girl who was sweet and sassy. She was also given to dramatic gestures, and in describing some terrible injustice she had heard about she would get caught up in her passion and sweep her arm about, knocking over whatever happened to be in her way.

My friend Leesie—Elise Bromberg—lived in a single-family house on Naples Road. It was a house filled with music and noise. Leesie, the youngest of three daughters, played the piano, but the others, including and especially her mother, Ann Bromberg, sang *Lieder* and operatic arias—dramatically and vigorously. And Burt Bromberg, Elise's father, was always there chatting, teasing, making bad jokes, and embarrasing his daughter literally to tears.

Sandy Simpson was a dancer; her family ran a dance school. She later became one of the Radio City Music Hall Rockettes. Lenore Mendelsohn lived across the street from Bobby. And in 1943, when we were nine years old, the two of us started playing war games. We convinced ourselves that there were spies at Coolidge Corner, probably in the barbershop, or maybe in the Chinese laundry. The fact that the Chinese were our allies did not impinge very much upon our callow sensibilities.

We devised a plan whereby we would spy on the spies. That meant lurking around the alley behind those stores to see what we could pick up. We eavesdropped. We picked through trash. We made up secret codes so that we could transmit our discoveries to each other—that is, should we ever discover anything. History will note that we tired of the game long before we could uncover any spies in our midst.

It was only recently that I learned, much to my amazement, that in fact Coolidge Corner had been a hotbed of spy activity during World War II. Just a few yards from where I had been skulking about in back alleys looking for spies, it turns out they had been there all the time. Only they were our guys.

Agents of the United States Counterintelligence Corps (CIC) were conducting spy business behind the facade of the Hoover Vacuum Cleaner Company. Checking security leaks and training other agents, these guys operated out of 325 Harvard Street, just two doors down from the Devotion School. A bronze plaque in front of my school playground attests to it.

I learned of this activity through the benign auspices of the Brookline Adult Education Thursday-night lecture series. "Spies Like Us: The Secret Life of Brookline's Counterintelligence Corps," an historical and anecdotal talk, was presented by Isadore Zack, president of the Military Intelligence Association of New England. Iz Zack had been my first boss when I went to work at the Anti-Defamation League of B'nai B'rith. Listening to him talk about the war years and the role he and his men had played —"We were not spies; we were spy catchers"—was fascinating. After his lecture, we greeted each other in the sweetest of reunions. It had been more than forty years since we last met, and we had a lot of catching up to do.

As a kid, I loved baseball. The game was a lifelong passion for my father. He would tell me of going to see the old Boston Americans when he was a boy and they played at the Huntington Avenue ballfield before Fenway Park was built in 1912. Going to Fenway Park with my dad was one of the great joys of my life. Does everyone remember the first time they went to a ball game? In the days before television, when there was only radio and the newspaper, the main image I had was not of sight, but of sound. I knew what the roar of the crowd was like, that vast sound that seemed to start in the belly of the crowd and lift up and up, like the balls my hero Ted Williams hit.

So I was unprepared for what the ballpark actually looked like and how it felt to be there. Entering through the turnstile into the dark, concrete netherworld beneath the field, my dad bought peanuts and a program. Making our way through the noisy crowd as I held my father's hand, we started up the ramp. We came out into the sunshine. It was better than I had imagined, beyond perfect.

The green grass of Fenway was the greenest green I had ever seen, the white uniforms of the Red Sox the whitest white imaginable. I can still hear the *thwack* of the ball as it sounded in the leather gloves as the team warmed up and the men tossed it to each other around the infield.

I read through the program. My father taught me how to read a batting average, how to keep score. I learned to make a little "x" in the space for a strikeout. I loved sitting in our seats at the ballpark, just the two of us, as my father tried to fathom why Dom DiMaggio would even consider bunting. "He should hit straight away, " my father would say, and I felt like his confidante, the recipient of this most privileged information.

Through the years I kept up my romance with baseball and with the Red Sox. When I was in high school, on opening day every year I would go to the game with my friends. By that time I had a serious crush on Ted Williams and kept a poster of him taped to the inside of my school locker. I knew his batting average; I read the sports page and fumed every time he was vilified by local sports writers. Watching him run in from left field, his head ducked down as he headed into the dugout, I didn't care that he refused to tip his hat to the fans; I was furious at the hecklers who sat in the left-field seats puposely to taunt him.

And then one day, it was over. And I wasn't in love anymore. Ted, the Splendid Splinter, had retired; I had grown up, and my father was gone. The Red Sox never won, indeed hadn't won a World Series since 1918 and our Boys of Summer seemed to me to be uninspired men just going through the motions. Starting full of hope every year, they faded every summer, when the cry from die-hard fans would be "wait 'til next year." I was no longer interested in or believed in next year. I had fallen in love with baseball because of the Red Sox, and I fell out of love with baseball because of the Red Sox.

I had good friends as I was growing up. Pretty, blue-eyed Sylvia Raymond was one. She was the youngest of four, with three older brothers, all of whom I thought were terribly handsome. Why, I would pester my parents, why didn't I have any brothers? I'd even take a sister if it was absolutely necessary. Couldn't they arrange it?

At one point during the war we came close to getting what I wanted. My mother was talking to my father about all the war orphans. So many children and so much suffering. They were being gathered up by humanitarian groups and housed in temporary barracks in Europe. There were many Jewish orphans. And one heard of the efforts on the part of Jewish agencies to bring them over to America for adoption. We could do that, couldn't we?

How serious the family conferences on the matter were, I don't know. Whether or not my parents ever investigated the possibility of adoption, I don't know. I only know that at some point I got wind of it and grew excited. I eagerly lobbied my parents on behalf of adoption. Boy, girl, young, old, I didn't care. Please, please, please, you have to do it, I begged. In the end nothing came of it. For me there was a fleeting sense of loss—probably for my parents as well. We all returned to our routines and never spoke of it again.

XVII. Victory

If not for the light, there would be no shadow.
  —*The Talmud*

WE WERE AT NANTASKET BEACH that summer of 1945. Our summer rentals at that seaside community fifty minutes south of Boston were sporadic and varied throughout the years of my childhood. We might stay anywhere from two weeks to the entire season, with my father going in to work every day and returning to us at night.

Nantasket Beach was in the town of Hull. It was a long strand of beach stretching miles up the Atlantic Coast. The main street was also called Nantasket Ave. (That's what we said; nobody ever called it "Avenue.")

I will never forget the ride to Nantasket and the excitement I felt about what lay ahead. From Brookline we drove through the old neighborhood of Morton Street and Blue Hill Avenue in Roxbury, past the Brown Derby Restaurant at the corner, just down from the G&G Delicatessen. Then on through Quincy and past the Baker Chocolate factory, where the aroma of chocolate made you giddy with desire.

We drove by Wollaston Beach, its waterfront filled with rocks so that if you ever stopped there for a swim, your mother made you wear rubber bathing shoes. Mine did. Then past Wollaston, past fried-clam shacks, past the first Howard Johnson's ice cream stand in the world. "Just a little further now" was the comforting answer to my impatient and incessant query, "How much longer?"

The sight that always quickened the heartbeat as we rounded the bend into Hull was huge and handsome, a sentinel of joy. The rollercoaster and Paragon Park, the premier amusement park in the Boston area. If summer was for promises "just around the bend," then the sight of that gladsome behemoth meant we had arrived in the Promised Land.

As we drove along Nantasket Ave, I soaked up all the familiar, delicious sights as they passed by one after another, each one filling me with memories and anticipation. We passed the first section of town called Kenberma where "nobody" stayed. But Kenberma was the home of the penny candy store. It was in Allerton that "everybody" stayed. This section of town was distinguished by its street names—the alphabet.

There was Abie's Delicatessen at A Street, its neon sign flashing. There was the L Street Theatre, the scene of so many summer movies and where I first saw *Gone with the Wind*. Priscilla's Chinese Restaurant at, I'm not sure, maybe H Street, served what was probably the worst, most popular Chinese food in the world. But that's not why people went there. Everyone went to Priscilla's for the blueberry pie, or, as it was universally known, "hot-ta-ta pie."

One year we rented rooms at a house on J Street. The owners were Italian and they had a wonderful toy, something I'd never seen before— an old player piano in the living room, and those lovely people allowed me to play it. I could sit for hours banging out "Heart of My Heart" and other old tunes, making believe I was really playing the piano as the rolls of music spun around and the piano keys went up and down as if ghostly hands were playing them.

There was the time, with my mother's sister Helen and her family, we rented on the bayside. I had my cousins Jan and Debby to play with as well as my friend Leesie, since we had taken rooms in the house the Bromberg family owned.

That summer was distinguished by some of Mr. Bromberg's escapades, one of which got us stranded out on his boat. He'd forgotten gas. As day turned to night we drifted aimlessly, not unduly concerned about our plight. We had to be towed in by the Coast Guard. Our anxious parents, their car headlights beacons of light from the shore, greeted us with such relief and with, I believe, a confirmation of their doubts as to poor Burt Bromberg's reliability.

As I got older, summer pleasures changed but never diminished. I progressed from pails and shovels and sand toys to jumping in the waves and learning to swim. Still ahead were dating and bonfires and picnics on the beach. So it was in the summer of 1945, when I was eleven, we were at Nantasket Beach. Franklin Roosevelt, who had sacrificed his life, his energies, and his health to shepherd the war through to victory, had died in April, just weeks short of the German surrender. Vice president Harry Truman—so little known, so little regarded then—succeeded to the presidency.

On May 8, V-E Day —commemorating victory in Europe—had been hailed in Paris and London, in Moscow and New York, as well as in every city and town across the country. The world knew then that the war in the Pacific would soon come to an end as well.

In Japan, during the first weeks of August, unprecedented and horrific events occurred. The fighting in the Pacific had intensified, and the Japanese, who had been determined to fight on to their death, never to surrender, were hit by a force never before seen in the world. An American bomber, the *Enola Gay*, dropped a new weapon, the atomic bomb, striking Hiroshima on August 6. Upwards of 100,000 people died in the devastating blast. The figures may even be greater, since thousands more were injured, many of whom would eventually die from their terrible wounds.

Still the Japanese did not surrender. On August 9, a second atomic bomb hit Nagasaki. Within hours of the blast, Emperor Hirohito and Japan's leaders knew there could be no hope of fighting on.

It was over. On Tuesday, August 14, victory was declared on what would forever after be known as V-J Day. Millions of people had lost their lives in the war. Russia alone suffered 10,000,000 civilian deaths and 10,000,000 military deaths. In Poland, 4,000,000 civilians lost their lives, as did 123,000 soldiers.*

The Nazi plan, known as the Final Solution, designed to rid the world of Jews, had been hideously successful. Six million Jews died in Europe as a result of Adolf Hitler's mad, genocidal policy.

The war had finally ended; the boys were coming home. Sirens wailed, factory whistles blared, church bells pealed; strangers wept and hugged and kissed and danced in the streets all over America. Two million people gathered in New York's Times Square. In Boston, the national anthem rang out from a speaker on top of the Liberty Mutual Building in Park Square. Motorists on nearby Boylston Street stopped their cars, got out, and stood at attention with their hands over their hearts, while servicemen on foot stood in rigid salute.

And in the little seaside community of Nantasket Beach, people honked their car horns, ran out in the streets, grabbed anyone they could and danced for joy. My father was hours late in reaching us from the city,

---

The Boston Globe. World War II Casualty Statistics Chart in August 14, 1995.

having been held up by traffic tie-ups as the streets of Boston—like those of towns all over the country—became clogged with happy revelers. But my father didn't have to worry about getting to work the next day, or even the day after. President Harry S Truman had declared August 15 and 16 national holidays. Victory—and peace. It was wonderful.

XVIII. Sweet Seventeen

My [elders] planted for me, and I planted for my children.
—*The Talmud*

NO SOONER HAD THE WAR ENDED, it seemed, that a new war began. Not a hot war, one of firepower and bombs, but a Cold War of ideology. The two most powerful nations on earth, America and the Soviet Union, were engaged in a struggle for supremacy. Russia's system of communism and militarism was pitted against our system of democracy and capitalism.

Russia was building up her military forces to the point where she would outstrip America in every category: Planes, troops, and tank divisions. But we had the bomb. We were the only nation on earth that had the atomic bomb. Yet in 1949, that too changed when Russia exploded its first A-bomb.

The thought of future wars fought not as they had been in the past with conventional weapons, but now with nuclear weapons, created a kind of fear the world had never known. It was unthinkable, people said, to ever contemplate war again. War—and certainly the weapons of war—must be outlawed. It was the only way to be safe in such a dangerous world. Others said we could not trust the Soviet Union, and if they have these weapons of devastation, then so too must we have them. That is the only way to be safe in such a dangerous world.

As I entered my teens, terrors such as these were not what I had on my mind. Whatever dangers lurked out there seemed rather abstract to me, although I certainly was no stranger to anxiety. But my concerns centered more on my own little world and how well I was faring in it. I was leaving behind grammar school and the life of a child, I was now a teenager and figured that life in Brookline was going to be about as much as I could handle.

I was thirteen and a freshman at Brookline High. Every day seemed an adventure. I made new friends; I found new activities in a school that offered everything from sports to drama to journalism. Never particularly athletic, I did, however "go out for" swimming and basketball, but only because some athletic activity was required if one was to earn an "Old English B," the pinnacle of Brookline High sports achievement. I was ambitious enough, but neither adept nor interested enough, and so fell short of earning my sports "B."

But if I wasn't going to be terrific in the sports arena—and I clearly wasn't—I could cast my eyes in other directions. Subscribing fully to the cheery, optimistic dictum that "the world is so full of a number of things, I'm sure we should all be as happy as kings," I found, indeed, numerous opportunities, ways to immerse myself in my new life.

Classes in English, social studies, Spanish, and the hated algebra certainly occupied me; I studied and did well. But life was outside of the classroom. You met your friends in the corridors, in the lunchroom, and after school in the quadrangle. And this being a time when good kids were not idle kids, I quickly got involved in what we called "extracurricular activities."

I was elected home room chairman, and I'm sure there were some attendant duties that came with the title, but I can't recall for the life of me what they might have been. The "responsibility" of this position propelled me toward other student government seats throughout my four years in high school.

By my senior year I had achieved the exalted status of president of the Girls League, the largest participatory club in school, whose motto was "Friendship, loyalty, and service." I had been elected to Alpha Pi, the school's honor society, where entrance was gained by scholastic points and extracurricular activity. And I was one of only three girls elected to the sixteen-member Student Council. The president of both the Honor Society and Student Council was Michael Dukakis.

Gertrude Stein, referring to the time she met Hemingway, remarked, "He was twenty-four; it was the time when everyone was twenty-four." She got it right. Only for me, it wasn't Paris in the 1920s; it was Brookline in 1951. I was seventeen, and it was the time when everyone was seventeen.

The faces that peer out from the pages of the high school yearbook appear smiling and cheerful. And remarkably neat. Even the members of the football team showed up for their class pictures wearing the requisite suits and ties. That is the way we were. We were also members of a senior class that numbered over 400. Our school, a four-year high school of approximately 1,800 students—the size of many a small college—was known for its academic excellence. Our town, with a population of about 55,000, was considered affluent, although that condition was not enjoyed by all.

We were in the French Club, the Dramatic Society, the Student Forum. The Student Council was described as "the voice of an active and spirited student body." Impressive words. But that's what the yearbook said, and that's what we believed. We were, after all, members of the decade before the sixties. No rebels, with or without a cause. No bumper-sticker sentiments exhorted us to "question authority." Our parents and teachers, the people who ran the world, seemed to us hopelessly dated, and yet we all aspired to join their ranks. And we had no doubt that when we did, we would do it better.

Who were we? We were children of immigrants who never thought of ourselves as such. Perhaps that is the ultimate triumph of our parents' and grandparents' struggle. We had achieved—in some cases in just a single generation—equality. We were American kids who took the same classes, studied the same books, and earned grades based on our ability, not on our names, our parents' incomes or our religion.

Who were we? There are sixteen kids in the School Council picture. We were Jewish, Irish, Italian, and Greek, all white and predominantly male. Some of our mothers were teachers, but most of our mothers were homemakers. Our fathers were salesmen or businessmen or, in a few cases, professionals. And out of that upwardly mobile tradition came sons and daughters who went off to Dartmouth and Tufts, Wellesley and Swarthmore.

No one, however, said "upwardly mobile" in the fifties, so it is with the hindsight and nomenclature of forty years later that one draws a group portrait in demographic terms. As teenagers we thought a lot about who we were, but it had far less to do with our parents and our backgrounds—or so we thought—than whether we were "cute" or "popular," the highest encomium one could garner.

The class distinction that really mattered to us was the esteem of our fellow students. The routes to high school success and achievement were mapped out by one's looks, brains, personality, and activism. Having just one of those attributes wasn't bad (unless it was brains), but having several was better. Having it all, of course, was the best. Some things never change.

Growing up when and where we did made us children of privilege.

No one in our group was wealthy—my dad spent a lifetime standing on his feet selling refrigerators at Jordan Marsh Company—but no one was poor either. No, we were privileged because we grew up in a time that was innocent and hopeful. Despite whatever personal agonies one suffered at the thought of being too short or too tall, too fat or too thin, of talking too much or of never knowing what to say, particularly to the opposite sex, most of us still retained an overriding belief in our own destiny. And that destiny—whatever it was—couldn't come soon enough for us.

XIX. Coming of Age

Be the master of your will and the slave of your conscience.
    —*Hassidic saying*

THE 1950s. THE NATION had come through the Roaring Twenties, the Depression thirties, and the war years of the forties. And somehow even through recovery and prosperity, the fifties brought the age of anxiety.

Taking society's pulse, the social commentators and prognosticators declared that as a nation we were definitely suffering from a bad case of the jitters. Nuclear power had been unleashed on the earth, and there was plenty to fear from the two superpowers, Russia and the United States.

At home, however, America was enjoying domestic growth and unparalleled prosperity. Dwight Eisenhower, the affable and popular World War II hero, was in the White House, and that made most people feel pretty good. We were in the middle of the American Century. The United States dominated the world in wealth, in productivity, and in influence. "There never was a country more fabulous than America," wrote British historian Robert Payne.

The decade of the fifties was a time of conformity and conventionality. But not for everyone. James Dean, who died in 1955, epitomized, in the handful of movies he made, the soulful, misunderstood rebel, a character and an actor that young America in particular took to its heart.

Writers Allen Ginsburg and Jack Kerouac gave voice to the Beat Generation, causing many of us to dream of life in the coffeehouses of Greenwich Village. The closest I ever came to the Bohemian life was to wear black, write turgid poetry, and drink espresso, which, no matter how I tried, I hated.

It was a time when there were still rules, rules that were often broken but nevertheless rules that everyone knew existed. Nobody wore jeans unless she lived in Wyoming. It was a time when dress codes still existed, and girls did not wear pants to school. The only words printed on tee-shirts were "Fruit of the Loom."

The rights of women, homosexuals, and the handicapped were non-issues. They were not discussed. Minorities struggled for equality. People didn't divorce; they stayed together "for the sake of the children."

There were no computers, CDs, calculators, car phones, color TVs or microwaves. There were no shopping malls. There was no profanity or nudity in films. Indeed, the Hollywood censors created a world that never was and never would be. Married couples were shown sleeping in twin beds as so decreed by the Breen Office, the overseer and final arbiter of movie morals in its day.

There were definite rules about sex. There was no such thing as legal abortion. You didn't kiss on a first date, and girls who "went all the way" were considered cheap. Nice girls didn't. Or if they did, they spent every moment from then on worrying about it.

This was the atmosphere in 1950, when I entered my senior year of high school. It is amazing to realize that despite all those limits on behavior and attitude we felt so free, unfettered, and happy.

I had an after-school job at a local music store, the only kind of selling job that interested me. Having been weaned on Hollywood musicals, one of my enduring fantasies was that I need only be in the right place at the right time in order to be "discovered." Didn't it happen in the movies all the time? And hadn't movie star Lana Turner been discovered sipping soda in a drugstore? I was not planning to hang out in drugstores all my life; I might as well be doing something useful in a promising place while I waited for my fate to unfold.

However, real-life music stores didn't seem to offer the same possibilities as movie music stores. I spent most of my time ringing up eighty-nine-cent sales on the cash register, the cost of a recording by a Vaughan Monroe or a Frank Sinatra. Still, while I never got discovered on the job, I found that I was doing some discovering of my own. Beecher Hobbs Company was a fine old establishment run by Mr. and Mrs. James Hobbs. The larger part of their business was in classical music. This was at a time when the record business was undergoing a revolution, both literally and figuratively. A symphony would most likely come in, say, four shellac 78-rpm discs boxed in an album, but these cumbersome items were on their way out to be replaced by the single long-playing, 33⅓-rpm record.

The other major seller for Beecher Hobbs was the Magnavox console record player, a big cabinet piece of furniture that housed a radio and record player. It was a classy thing—top of the line—coveted by many, above all by those who recognized quality, as Mr. Hobbs stated often with something akin to religious fervor.

Only Mr. Hobbs dealt with customers interested in the Magnavox. White-haired, tall but slightly stooped, he was the epitome of Yankee propriety. He had a slightly distracted air about him, as if when he picked his head up and looked around, he was surprised to find himself there—or anywhere. He was a lovely and gentle soul.

Mrs. Hobbs was different. More solid and down-to-earth, her thoughts were never elsewhere; she was here, she was in charge, and she made you know it. My function was to tend to our valued customers only if no one else of greater maturity and importance was on the premises. I also did the occasional window display and wielded the feather duster to keep the records clean.

What they really hired me—"the girl"—for was to sell the records that the teenagers coveted. The music and the kids seemed utterly alien to both Mr. and Mrs. Hobbs. But if I had to write an essay along the lines of "What I Learned on My Summer Vacation," I would say that what I learned at Beecher Hobbs was *life*, or at least what I thought was life. For in addition to Mr. and Mrs. Hobbs, there were two other employees.

Both Paul Deane and Connie Eldred were older than I. They were in their twenties, they were friends and colleagues, each married, Paul to friendly, red-headed Betty, and Connie to the remote Ken. They were unlike any grownups I had ever known, not parent or teacher or authority figure. They were *adults* who became my friends.

Why Connie and Paul paid any attention to me I will never know. But they did. In fact, they took me under their wings and introduced me to the world of books and ideas. At lunchtime, in the office loft above the shop, they read magazines like *The Saturday Review of Literature* and then *talked* about what they read. I listened. And learned. To me, Connie and Paul were paradigms of sophistication and everything I hoped to be—no, everything I *planned* to be.

Paul was an avid movie fan, but not in the way I was. I couldn't imagine Paul buying copies of *Modern Screen* and snipping out photos of John Payne or Alan Ladd to hang on the wall. No, he analyzed the films and discussed them. These thoughtful, intellectual people opened up doors for me that I never even knew existed.

I volunteered in Boston at a settlement house with my friend Elaine

Goldman, going in every Saturday morning to work with young children. Connie, who lived in the South End, had an interest in community work, and I often went to a Settlement House there with her. Of course I was flattered by her interest in me, believing that I was more mature than others my age and therefore worthy of her attention. Very likely, Connie—and Paul to a lesser degree—was also flattered by an impressionable teenager who hung on her every word.

When I wasn't going home with reading lists from Connie and Paul—they argued over whether I should start F. Scott Fitzgerald by reading *The Beautiful and the Damned* or *The Great Gatsby* (*Gatsby* lost out)—I was happily involved in my high school "career." For one thing, I was part of a singing trio. We were a big hit entertaining at sweet sixteen parties, known far and wide, at least from North Brookline to South Brookline. Elaine Goldman, Laura Schnitzler, and I were the happy troubadours, no doubt delighting ourselves more than our audiences with such tunes as "Sentimental Journey." Besides our musicality, we were serious about choreographing songs like that one, spending many afternoons rehearsing, pumping our arms to simulate railroad trains chugging down the tracks.

During the fifties I graduated high school, briefly entertained the thought of going to New York in order to pursue a career in the theater, then abandoned that dream. I had fallen in love.

He was tall, dark, and handsome. And he was smart. Alan Rothstein had grown up in Brookline; in fact, we had gone to the same schools. Now he was in college, pre-med. He had always wanted to be a doctor, a psychiatrist. He was different from anyone I'd ever known: complex, a little detached, impatient. I believed then, as I do now, that he was the most generous, resourceful, and unselfish person I ever met. But he had deep and private places where no one had ever gone before; they would be hard to penetrate.

Alan made me laugh with his dry and often mordant sense of humor. He taught me how to parallel park; he told me things about the scientific world I'd never even thought about.

I knew that he had uncommon strength, even courage. He went about his business with a determination that never allowed for any quitting or whining. So I was not surprised when one day, many years later on holiday in Spain, he chased a purse-snatcher down a street in Seville, or on that terrible day at Boston State Hospital when he braved a gun-wielding madman in an effort to save a mortally wounded colleague, who, tragically would die of his wounds weeks later.

Alan had an enormous capacity to look at life unvarnished and no capacity whatsoever for wistful dreams and fantasies. His upbringing certainly had a lot to do with that.

He was raised by his paternal grandparents and by his father's sister and her husband. Alan's mother had been hospitalized with schizophrenia, having suffered a breakdown only months after he was born. His father was remarried and saw his son so infrequently as to be only a shadow figure throughout Alan's early years.

"How sad," I remarked when learning these facts, "how tragic."

"Not at all," said Alan, with what I would come to recognize as his typical lack of sentimentality. "I was raised with good people who loved me. No, I was lucky."

Our courtship was about discovery, as courtship always is. Alan shared with me a confidence in ourselves and in our future. We were motivated by youthful ideals and a belief in a better world. We read *The Nation*, an ultra-liberal weekly periodical. I took out a subscription to *Ebony* magazine and joined the National Association for the Advancement of Colored People (NAACP). I'm ashamed to admit how proud I was of myself.

We went to foreign films. That was very avant-garde in the fifties. We particularly liked the English comedies starring Alec Guiness. We went to dark, smoke-filled nightclubs to listen to jazz. Sipping cokes and smoking Chesterfield cigarettes, we tapped our feet and fell in love with the Dixieland sound of Jimmy Archey's band at the Savoy.

We cried with folk singer Josh White at Storyville as he sang "Strange Fruit," a bitter, heart-breaking song about the lynching of American negroes in the Deep South. And we laughed at the silliness and fun of Slim Gaillard at the High-Hat singing "Cement Mixer, Putty Putty." Somehow all these things, innocent as they were, seemed very daring. They were things our parents didn't do.

We went to church, too. My parents, of course, were horrified. Alan and I started attending the Sunday morning lectures at the Community Church in Boston. All the years Karla and I were growing up, it had never occurred to me to go hear her father speak at his church. But now Reverend Lothrop seemed to me the very model of the honorable liberal, valiantly fighting the good fight of enlightenment. Carey McWilliams of *The Nation* spoke there, as did other liberals trying to alert their audiences to the dangers of apathy and bigotry.

The presidential election of 1952 seemed part of a bigger world, the world I yearned to belong to. Though I would marry in 1953 at the age of nineteen, in that election year of '52 I was only eighteen and not old enough to vote. Still, I wasn't going to sit the election out. As I knocked on doors passing out campaign literature for Adlai Stevenson, the Democratic candidate for president, I had no way of knowing that I was beginning a lifetime of political campaigning, of addressing and licking envelopes and driving voters to the polls, of phoning and organizing. Stevenson's influence was an awakening for me, as it was for millions of others. But, judging by the final election figures, not enough others.

Here was a man we could believe in, someone whose eloquence and brilliance thrilled us, who made us feel that government could and should care for those least able to care for themselves. But nothing would stop the juggernaut that was Dwight D. Eisenhower. War hero of the forties, he was an avuncular avatar of benign prosperity in the fifties. As writer David Halberstam put it, "If Stevenson was the candidate of the readers of *The New Yorker*, *Harper's* and the *Atlantic*, then…Ike was the candidate of the *Saturday Evening Post* and *Reader's Digest*."[*] No contest.

On election night 1952, as Alan and I watched our candidate lose, we cried the tears of defeat. My parents had voted for Eisenhower. Everybody, it seemed, liked Ike.

Stevenson remained a hero to those of us who believed in a government whose leaders could be people of integrity, intelligence, even humor. Another gentleman was about to emerge who exhibited many of those same qualities. Courtly and humane, a short and balding Boston attorney named Joseph Welch mesmerized a nation that had been held too long in the thrall of the senator from Wisconsin, Joseph McCarthy.

McCarthy, under the guise of uncovering communists, was a demagogue, guilty of the worst kind of character assassination. Joe McCarthy whose name itself, in the form of "McCarthyism," came to represent the evils of right-wing extremism, was guilty of costing people their reputations, their livelihoods and, in some instances, their lives. Even to be suspected of communism was enough to put your name on the black list, meaning that you would not be hired. In such an atmosphere, suicide was not uncommon.

----

[*]Halberstam, David. *The Fifties*. p. 116.

XX. The Fifties

When a man appears before the Throne of Judgment, the first question he is asked is, "Have you dealt honorably and faithfully in all your dealings with your fellowman?"

—*The Talmud*

IN APRIL OF 1954, MARRIED TEN MONTHS, my husband in his second year of medical school, I had just given birth to our first child, Peter Harris Rothstein. "Your little boy has everything he should have," pronounced my wonderful doctor, David Kopans, "and nothing he shouldn't have." Glorious words for one of life's best moments.

I had been working at The Anti-Defamation League of B'nai B'rith. Propelled by the romantic notion that I couldn't go to work "just any-where" and that a social justice agency, particularly one dedicated to fighting anti-Semitism, would be right for me, I took the job working for the Civil Rights Director, Isadore Zack.

Iz Zack was a man whose generous disposition matched his large frame, and whose sense of humor was coupled with a sense of the absurd. How else to explain his turning me loose on Father Feeney? "Go on down to the Common, kid," he'd tell me, instructing me to mingle with the Sunday crowd on Boston Common and take notes as the excommuni-cated anti-Semitic priest spewed his message of soap-box hatred.

Feeling distinctly like some two-bit gumshoe, I would circulate around the edges of the crowd, furtively taking notes that I would later write up into a report to be put on Iz Zack's desk the next day. Keeping tabs on what the haters were saying was part of the ADL's fact-finding program. You couldn't tell the haters without a score card, and we were definitely keeping score.

But in April of 1954 I was a brand-new mother, home from the hospital, settled in before the television set with twenty million other Americans to watch the Army-McCarthy hearings. The senator had had his way far too long, intimidating most of the nation's press and politicians by wrapping himself in the cloak of patriotism as he made his unfounded and never-to-be-proven charges of communism in government.

The Army-McCarthy hearings were ostensibly taking place to air charges about communists in the military and counter-charges that McCarthy was trying to blackmail the Army in order to advance the Army career of his protégé, one G. David Schine. This was the O.J. Simpson trial of its day, with an audience alternately repelled and fascinated. McCarthy had a nasty habit of defaming people without any regard for truth or justice. Then, one day, he went too far.

"I think we should tell Mr. Welch that he has in his law firm," Senator McCarthy unctuously intoned, "a young man named Fisher who has been for a number of years a member of an organization named as the legal bulwark of the Communist Party...."

The picture of the gentle Boston attorney Joseph Welch holding his hand to his forehead, tight-lipped, eyes downcast as he listened to a vicious character assassination was more compelling than anything the television audience had ever seen. But the words he spoke would prove even more riveting.

"Until this moment, Senator, I think I never really gauged your cruelty or your recklessness. Fred Fisher is starting what looks to be a brilliant career with us. Little did I dream you could be so reckless and so cruel as to do an injury to that lad. I fear he shall always bear a scar needlessly inflicted by you.... Let us not assassinate this lad further, Senator. You have done enough. Have you no sense of decency, sir, at long last? Have you left no sense of decency?"

It was over. Oh, the hearings droned on a little longer; so did McCarthy. But he was finished. He knew it. Every American watching knew it. The press knew it. Everyone in government knew it. And to think that he was brought down by a kindly, honest, and very decent gentleman from Boston.

In December of 1954 McCarthy was condemned by his senate colleagues in a formal vote. Three years later he was dead of alcohol-related liver disease.

Other things were happening in the world. In 1953, with the release of *Sexual Behavior in the Human Female*, or as it became universally known, "The Kinsey Report," named after its author, Indiana University college professor Alfred Kinsey, the country responded with equal parts approval and criticism. "Of course, Dr. Kinsey's right," said his supporters. "His data shows what we've always known: there is such a thing as premarital and extramarital sex."

His critics, on the other hand, condemned the study, believing it to signal the deterioration of morals in America—an opinion no doubt exacerbated by the emergence of a new magazine called *Playboy*, a male fantasy-come-true and a nightmare for straight-laced sexual Victorians.

For those who believed that the country was going to hell in a hand basket, there was further confirmation of their fears in the new music that had burst onto the scene. Surely the nation's youth was rollicking down that rocky road to ruin as they danced and sang to rock 'n' roll. But what was a vulgar and degrading spectacle for some, was for others exciting, new and fabulous.

Ballads, sweet-sounding love songs made popular by singers such as Frank Sinatra, Doris Day, and Rosemary Clooney, had been around forever. It was America's music, loved by everyone. But there was also more exhilarating, lively music in the pop vein: swing, jazz, boogie-woogie.

Much of this great sound came from black musicians. But in the fifties racist attitudes still dominated, and the only one who really had a chance to popularize the new music would be, say, a nice, modest white boy from the south. Waiting in the wings was just such a young man from Memphis named Elvis Presley.

It began in 1955 with Bill Haley and the Comets doing a little number called "Rock Around the Clock." Elvis had two best-selling hits the next year, "Don't Be Cruel" and "Heartbreak Hotel." Kids went crazy with the excitement of the sounds, and the new "fad" of rock 'n' roll became a permanent addition to the music scene.

On Broadway, *My Fair Lady*, with a little-known British actress named Julie Andrews, became an enormous hit. So too did Leonard Bernstein's *West Side Story*, an updating of the Romeo and Juliet saga told against contemporary New York Puerto Rican society.

A housewife from New Hampshire wrote the best-selling novel of the decade, *Peyton Place*, a tale of sexual intrigue in small-town America. J.D. Salinger's novel *Catcher in the Rye* became an instant hit, and its story of youthful alienation would be an enduring classic.

But if you asked anyone what they were doing in the fifties, the answer—if it was Tuesday night—was "Watching Uncle Miltie." Milton Berle, a vaudeville comic and entertainer with funny costumes and even funnier faces "owned" Tuesday night, when millions of Americans tuned in to watch his hilarious antics on the Texaco Star Theater. No wonder he came to be known as "Mr. Television." And if there was a "Mrs. Television," surely it was Lucy. Lucille Ball, star of *I Love Lucy*, appeared in a half-hour comedy show that is still being shown in reruns and which, in fact, has never been off the air since it began in 1951.

1956 was the second time around for Adlai Stevenson as well as for Alan and me. It turned out that we were a good deal luckier than Stevenson; he lost his second bid for the presidency, while Alan and I had another "perfect" baby boy, Steven. He was born with laughing eyes and a full head of lustrous black curls. We were overjoyed, an emotion almost unanimously felt.

At first Peter exhibited a certain natural wariness at the prospect of this new baby, this interloper. He dealt with the situation in a forthright manner: he refused to talk to the obvious source of his annoyance, me. And, I recall, his silent treatment lasted for about twenty-four hours, during which time he became increasingly interested in and enamored of his baby brother.

We lived in Indianapolis that year, the year of Alan's medical internship, during one of the worst polio epidemics to ever hit the Midwest. By the end of the decade we had returned east and were launched on even further travels. On Halloween night 1959 my boys and I flew across the Atlantic to Germany. Five-year-old Peter had the time of his life drinking cocoa and visiting in the cockpit with the pilot. Three-year-old Steven threw up half the way across the ocean. His handsome jacket and clip-on bow tie did not fare well in the ordeal.

We were joining Alan, now Captain Rothstein. He had been drafted into the Army and though we'd only been apart three weeks, we were anxious to be together in our new home. For the next two years that would be in Germany, in a village called Weiersbach. How strange and unfamiliar it all seemed. Except for one thing which felt very right: we were again expecting a new baby.

XXI. Germany

God prefers your deeds to your ancestors' virtues.

—*Genesis*

GERMANY. THERE HAD BEEN some choice in the matter—not a lot, but some. Alan had been drafted and would have to serve in the Army for two years; there was no choice about that. But he did have the option to request overseas duty. There was no guarantee, of course, that such a request would be honored. However, if we asked for Europe and got it, we knew that in all likelihood we'd be going to Germany, where the majority of the Army troops were stationed.

We had long discussions—were they rationalizations?—about Germany. It was only a dozen years or so after the end of World War II; could we, as Jews, go and live in a country whose wartime leaders had murdered millions of our people? But for the accident of birth, Alan and I, our families, and our loved ones would almost surely have been among the six million European Jews who met their deaths at the hands of Nazi exterminators.

We talked about it and around it and through it until we got to the point of saying "let's do it." We wanted to travel; we wanted to go to Europe, and we wanted the experience of living abroad. We might just have a chance to do all that courtesy of the United States Army.

It was a blistering summer in San Antonio, Texas. We had a tiny apartment and settled in for Alan's six-week basic training. As we came to the end of that training period, everyone got more anxious. Alan and every man in the group wondered, "Where will I be sent?" When the day came that assignments were posted, we found that about one third of Alan's group was going to Korea. Alan's orders came for the 98th General

Hospital in Neubruecke, Germany.

We couldn't even find it on the map. It was somewhere in the Rhine-land Palatinate, the region that forms a link between the Saarland to the west and the Rhineland to the east. We knew that somewhere between the vineyard town of Bernkastel and the oldest city in Germany, Trier, somewhere there, smack in the middle, was us. That was where we were going.

Alan made his way alone to Fort Dix in New Jersey. How soon be-fore we would be together again? His letters were full of the routines of Army life, of briefing sessions and life in the barracks. "There is absolute-ly nothing else we have to do here except check a list three times a day for our departure orders.... I miss my family."

Arriving in Germany, he wrote that it was "isolated and very rural, but, you'll see, it's going to be wonderful...."

Finding a place for us to live was his main priority. Finally, he wrote that there was a good place in the neighboring village of Weiersbach, and unlike other houses he had seen, this one had heat and hot water and in-door plumbing. It was a one-family house, but the people who owned it and who lived downstairs rented out the top floor as an apartment. It had a kitchen, two bedrooms, a living room/dining area, and a bathroom. "It only has a toilet right now," Alan wrote, "but Herr Hoenig plans to put in a sink soon.... The Hoenigs are charming people." Despite the assur-ances, I felt some anxiety.

Willi Hoenig worked for the railroad. His wife was Nelly. Her father ran the local pub, or *Gasthaus*, and hers was the only Protestant family in this all-Catholic village.

Only the downstairs bathroom has a bath," Alan wrote, "but don't worry.... A few things we may do without, but we'll all be together.... It'll be a wonderful experience for the children with fields and farms to play in; just today I saw some of the village kids happily digging up po-tatoes in the field... and there's a kindergarten just down the road.... We don't have to prolong this separation any longer. I've rented the rooms—it's $85 a month—so, please, please get your passport and your plane reservations and come...."

Nelly and Willi Hoenig had built a solid, sturdy home of unpainted cinder block. A curved dirt road led to the house, which stood out against the cold, gray landscape of field and trees. The Hoenigs were lined up at the door anxiously anticipating our arrival.

Nelly, small with a ruddy complexion and warm, dark eyes that seemed to miss nothing, was there to greet us as the boys and I entered with Alan. Willi, tall and broad-shouldered, had blue eyes that shone out of a playful, open face. Their children, Rita and Marlene, nine and eight years old, grinned shyly at us as they peered out, half-hidden, from behind their mother. We all smiled and nodded a great deal, with many utterances of *"Wilkommen"* and *"Danke schoen"* echoing through the hall. Our grasp of German was as tenuous as theirs was of English. It was clear that we would be living in close proximity; not even a door divided the second floor from the first. How would we get along? Would we like each other?

Three years later, back in America, a letter from Nelly described the American family who succeeded us. They had a boy, she wrote, who *"ist so alt wie Steven, als ihr zu uns kamt"* (is as old as Steven was when you came to us). *"Der untershied ist wie Sonne und Mond. Er ist schlimm...."* (The difference is like the sun and the moon; this is a bad boy....)

Nelly, Willi, and Alan were all talking at once, trying to explain the bathing situation to me. During the winter there would be hot water every day. But come summer, the furnace would only be fired up once a week; thus there would be hot water only once a week. The boys could hardly believe their good fortune. A bath only once a week; paradise!

We were tired. It had been a long three-hour ride from Frankfurt, a journey we made with another American family. Gene Yurich of Wisconsin was the ear, nose, and throat doctor at the 98th General Hospital. Alan had met him when they arrived at their new post within a day of each other. Both Alan and Gene had spent time looking for housing for their families while getting familiar with their new professional and military duties. They had become friends.

Gene's wife, Joan, arrived in Frankfurt with their two little boys, Michael and Jimmy, on the same day we did. After a night's sleep at the base, the two families met for the first time, and we enacted our own version of pioneers trekking west in a covered wagon—a borrowed Chevy, in our case.

We were eight people: two pregnant women, four boys ages one to five, two brand-new captains in the United States Army, and five pieces of luggage. It was snug. The only thing missing was a partridge in a pear tree. We established an instant friendship with the Yurichs. The similarity of our situations, our mutual uncertainties concerning our coming adventure, the two years ahead of us, and the fact that we were to be neighbors all meant that by the time we arrived at our village of Weiersbach, we had forged close ties, ones that would remain throughout our time together in the Army.

Gene had found a place for his family across the road from us. It too was a crude, unpainted cinderblock. But it was also more—or less. Surveying her new home for the first time, Joan experienced serious culture shock as she stared at the mud oozing in the yard and at the chickens stalking about imperiously. She smiled a wobbly little grin. When one of the kids asked, "What smells like that?" the smile seemed to slip a bit.

The pungent aroma emanated from the "honey pile," the mound of hay and manure standing to the left of their front door. When we learned that pigs were cured in the attic and chickens kept in the cellar, we didn't know what else to do except hug the Yurichs and wish them good luck.

XXII. Village Life

Yet, I keep [my ideals], because in spite of everything I still believe that people are really good at heart.

—Anne Frank

I WAS A STRANGER IN A STRANGE LAND. And somehow I was not as prepared for it as I thought. The adjustment was different for each of us. Alan's days were spent at the hospital—an Army hospital, but more or less familiar territory for him. The world of childhood is the same in whatever territory it finds itself and so our boys ran, played, and laughed as they always had. Only I seemed to be gingerly poking around the edges.

I thought about the discussions we had had before coming to Germany, and how we had probed the deep, black waters of Germany and the Nazis, how we felt a horror that could never change. Yet we felt other things too. There was a curiosity, even a sense of adventure, and a pragmatic consideration: how—or when—could we ever manage to take our children and live abroad for two years? For two people who had never been out of the country, this was a definite attraction.

Still, the tug-of-war with our sensibilities continued. We had told ourselves that the sins of the fathers should not be visited upon their descendants. The trouble was, many of the "fathers" of the Third Reich were still around. Some were our neighbors. After all the war had ended only fourteen years before. I was to discover that I would never completely reconcile my conflicting feelings.

There was the very real kindness of the Hoenig family juxtaposed with the grimness of the surroundings, always tinged by the past. There was the old man across the road who sat and rocked in his rocking chair

157

and who stared silently at us as we walked by his porch—a former Gestapo man, we were told.

There was the gas station at the corner, owned and operated by the German family who had taken it over when the former Jewish owners were taken away. Down by the Bahnhof, the train station, we stared at the apartment building that used to be a synagogue, its faint Star of David still discernible.

Sometimes when I saw the impassive faces of so many of the villagers, I wondered if they even knew we were Jewish. Though I felt their coolness was based on anti-Semitism, it could have been mere indifference. Maybe they didn't like us because we were Americans, foreigners, *"Auslaender."* After all, we were the occupying army. Throughout history, that has been a pretty good reason for resentment.

But the children: I had only to look out the window to see my little boys scampering about in play with their new friends. None of these children—not ours, not theirs—had known hatred or terror, and one hopes they never will.

But someday I want them to know and remember what happened here. Not so that it will breed hate and fear, but in order to keep faith by remembering. Is it too naive to believe that memory and understanding might keep such horrors from ever happening again?

Peter, Steven, Marlene, and Rita got along marvelously. They were good children, friendly, respectful, and eager. They had little difficulty in overcoming the language barrier. Giggling, *spieling* board games, responding to invitations from Peter and Steven to *"kommen sie* up to play," Marlene and Rita eagerly replied, "Yes, we come!"

Nelly and Willi were not a farming family—Willi worked for the railroad—and in that respect they were unique in Weiersbach. They seemed to enjoy special status in this hard-scrabble farming community. I think Nelly felt somewhat superior to the women at work in the fields—so many women without men, yet another reminder of the devastation of war. Dressed in heavy black stockings, gray woolen skirts covered by aprons, and wearing the ubiquitous sweaters and babushkas, these women also wore a look of resignation and bitterness.

Life in farm country teaches quite a lot, I could see. Children learn very directly and immediately about life, death, and work. Peter's class at the *Kinderschule* took a field trip to the cemetery, he reported, where they sang *"Kindertotenlieder,"* songs for dead children. Not the usual American outing to the fire station.

Another day, the boys and I watched as the farmer across the road watered his field the old-fashioned way. He had an ox-driven cart that held water tanks. The farmer gave the oxen the whip after loosening the caps from the tanks so that the water spilled out as the animals lumbered along. The farmer then ran alongside the cart to make sure that irrigation occurred at regular intervals.

Life was very basic, even primitive. But it was very direct and understandable for children. There was an action and a reaction. Explain to a city child that milk comes from a cow rather than from the carton they pick up in the supermarket. Here, they see. My boys went down the road to the lady who kept cows. They carried a tin cup, handed it to her, she pulled at her cow and there it was: milk.

Life was very real in Weiersbach. Sometimes too real. There was the day the bomb was discovered. Lying dormant since the war, it was found by some children over by the *Kinderschule*, under the bridge across the Nahe River, where my boys walked every day on their way to school. The bomb was dismantled, defused, and removed amid an atmosphere that was something akin to a school holiday—at least for the children of Weiersbach.

The local baker came by with his truck three times a week. Standing outside with a sweater thrown over my shoulders to ward off the morning chill, I shivered in the gray cold of the air, taking in the warm smell of the breads. The big black bread was my favorite. We had it at supper with a bottle of wine that Nelly brought us from her father's *Gasthaus*. It cost one Deutschmark a bottle, the equivalent of twenty-five cents.

Alan and Willi took the four children to the *Gasthaus* for a visit. While the papas had beer, the children watched some television. We had no TV at the house, but the Hoenigs did downstairs. The boys were delighted to see that Lloyd Bridges could swim underwater in German as well as he did in English.

We started to settle into a comfortable domestic arrangement with the Hoenigs. Often in the evening we played a cardgame called Flinch. It was a silly enough game and the only one we all knew that didn't tax our linguistic abilities beyond their capacities.

Willi became like a favorite uncle to the boys. They eagerly awaited his return home from work at day's end, when they might then plant fruit trees out back. Willi would dig a hole and allow the boys to each tip a spadeful of dirt over. He carefully showed them how to lift and place the infant tree into place.

One time Alan and I had been reading Dickens' *A Christmas Carol* to the boys, and then the story was presented on television. Nelly and Willi invited us down with Peter and Steven to watch it. Steven, who has fallen asleep on dinner tables, floors, and other assorted venues, promptly fell asleep before the TV. Willi carried him up to bed. The next morning he affectionately teased Steven by telling him it was the ghost [of Christmas future?] who had taken him upstairs. Looking at Willi's jolly face, our little boy laughed and said, *"Du bist der Geist, ich weißt!"* (You are the ghost, I know!)

A cultural exchange of sorts seemed to take place between the children. It soon became apparent that when Rita and Marlene left the house, they called, "Bye-bye, Mama." When our boys went out to play, their parting words were *"Wiederseh'n,* Mama."

Nelly was very kind and helpful. When I mentioned to her that I would like to get some help with the baby coming soon, before I knew it a fine, strong-looking woman named Anna Kirsch appeared. Anna, who would be such an important part of our lives, seemed, even at first meeting, to be a combination of Mary Poppins and Popeye the Sailor Man. She was, indeed, a person of many parts. She had several part-time jobs in the village. Beginning at seven o'clock each morning she dashed—Anna never walked if she could dash, run, or barrel along—to the schoolhouse to fire up the furnace. Each night at five thirty she was back there to clean up.

Anna told the boys she would play with them if they were good, and she promised to show them how to chop wood, play hide-and-seek, and whistle. Did I say Mary Poppins? She was better than Mary Poppins.

In addition to conflicting sensibilities and kind-hearted people who befriended us, we had other lessons to learn about life in a small German village. As Americans we were used to creature comforts, convinced that they were our right and privilege. In Weiersbach we lived on a dirt road that became a muddy river during the frequent rains. We had to share bathing facilities with our landlords, and with only two bedrooms, our children—soon to be three—would have to share a single room. In the beginning we had no phone and no car. But when we had no water, that's when we got mad.

At first we were patient, acknowledging that a little deprivation was good for the soul. After all, modern conveniences are just that: modern and convenient. It's only recently that they've even been around, and still that's only for some of us. Lots of people throughout the world must manage without conveniences. But after three days of no water for brushing one's teeth or flushing the toilet, such rationalizations—well, they didn't hold water.

We had thought that the frequent rains would alleviate the drought everyone talked about. But we were wrong. It seems that the town well had diminished reserves, and the mayor, or *Burgermeister*, without warning or notification, just shut off all water.

Some people said that another well could easily be built. Apparently there was water on the school property, and there had been a lot of haggling with the teachers, who were definitely not interested in selling their land to the village. Somehow no one seemed to have given thought to seeking water elsewhere.

That's what we did. We sought—and found—another source for water. The hospital had water, and Alan brought home five-gallon jugs that we parceled out in buckets to be used—sparingly—for the necessities.

Beyond the village life in Weiersbach there was another life, that of the Army. It was very social, and yet quite stratified. There were parties and get-togethers; the Officers' Club hosted a daily happy hour, and it seemed always to be like Friday night at the frat house.

Army society was different from anything I'd ever known. There was no fraternization between officers and enlisted men, from what I could see. And there was a separation also between career officers and the two-year people like us. The career people were like junior executives, extolling the virtues and rewards of company life. As for us two-year people, we were guilty of being a bit smug, of relishing our individuality as we passed through military service before returning to "real life" in the "real world."

Other layers in the crazy-quilt tapestry of village life emerged as our family got caught up in local customs. St. Nicholas Nacht arrived, and the four children of our household were in a state of nervous frenzy. Nelly had prepared us for what would take place, but I still would not have believed it had I not seen it with my own eyes.

Four fidgety children sat on the couch in the Hoenig living room when old St. Nicholas, making his way to each household in the village, appeared in the doorway. With his flowing white beard and familiar red costume, he stood before the children reading from his ledger.

"Have you been drinking your milk? Have you been fighting with your brother or sister?" There were only positive answers in this household, so after a spirited rendition of "O, Tannenbaum" and the distribution of goody bags, the good gentleman went on his merry way.

But there was more to come. The bell rang, and the children knew what this meant. The Swartz Mann had arrived. A more frightening apparition would be hard to imagine. He came in crawling on all fours, dressed in black from head to toe. His face was partially covered by a dark scarf, his hands were blackened with soot, and he had a heavy chain draped across his chest. He carried a straw switch in one hand. The children clung to each other, their eyes wide, as Nelly, acting out her part of the drama, blocked the Swartz Mann's entry into the room, assuring him that only good children lived here. He turned around and retreated, issuing a few departing growls and snarls.

Over wine and refreshments, Nelly described to us how some parents actually let the Swartz Mann go so far as to put a naughty child into his sack. At this point a lifetime promise of good behavior would easily be extracted from the terrified child. Naturally we were horrified and could only imagine what Dr. Spock would make of this.

Peter and Steven attended the afternoon session of the *Kinderschule*. Run by the kindly nuns and headed by Sister Bertrama, the school was only a few minutes from the house. There were about sixty children there, ranging in age from two to seven. Maybe ten of them were Americans.

As our boys headed home at four thirty carrying their lunch boxes, they were part of a long single line of children trudging along the road past fields and farmhouses. Watching from the window of the house, I witnessed their recessional as they solemnly bowed, shaking hands with the sisters before breaking into a run as they made for home.

Since they never brought home drawings or papers, I asked Peter, "What do you do all day?"

"All we do is play and pray, play and pray," he said. Surely an answer worthy of a permanent place in the family annals.

Weiersbach, 1960
Our apartment was on the
second floor of the house on the right

Village life in Weiersbach

Steven and Peter Rothstein and Rita and Marlene Hoenig get a visit from St. Nicholas and the Schwartz Mann in Wiersbach

Anna Kirsch

XXIII. Anna

As others planted before me, so do I plant for my children.

—The Talmud

OUR LEAP-YEAR BABY, our daughter Katie, arrived on February 29, 1960. Overjoyed and overwhelmed with love for her, we found that getting used to another child and having a baby around the house was so easy that it was hard to believe. I had worried about disturbing the Hoenigs downstairs, but Katie was, as they immediately declared, *"immer gute."*

Anna was mad for the baby. We found from the start that Anna had moved into the bosom of our family and taken us over. She claimed us for her own, and we could no more have prevented it than we could have altered the sun from its course. There she would be, swooping down on us with her booming laugh and spiriting the children off to one place or another. They visited Anna's friends, where they were invited to partake of cakes and coffee, or they stopped at the *Gasthaus* to watch a little television.

One day when the boys didn't feel like going to *Kinderschule*, Anna grabbed her coat and, before they knew what hit them she boomed out, "Come! Anna goes to school today too." And just like that they were gone: walking off, holding hands, and definitely going to school. They never stood a chance.

Peter had taken to going next door to help our neighbor, who was at work building his house. Loading the wheelbarrow with dirt and bricks, Peter worked tirelessly until finally Herr Hauser said, *"Genug."* The house, practically a twin to ours, was two stories, with a peaked roof but lacking indoor plumbing.

One day Sister Bertrama came calling. "The Sister has come to see my sister," Steven kept saying over and over, thrilled with the honor of such an important visitor. Fat and jolly, she came puffing up the stairs, toting little Easter baskets stuffed with candy for the boys.

Each of them shook hands with the Sister, thanking her for the gifts and then proudly escorted her to see their baby or the *"kleine Katerina,"* as the Sister dubbed her. Over tea Sister Bertrama told lovely stories about my boys, of Peter's friendship with his "good *Kamarad*, Wolfgang," and of Steven's happy grin and laughing ways.

No sooner did the good Sister depart then the *Krankenschwester* (nurse) arrived. This Sister tends to the sick, the *Krankenhaus* being attached to the *Kinderschule* so that everyone—young, old, sick, well, everyone—is connected. It certainly seems a radical idea, sounding suspiciously like a family.

Anna was at our home practically *"jeden Tag"* (every day). Even on Good Friday she insisted upon coming for the morning and doing the laundry. Her one concession to the solemnity of the day was that she hung the clothes indoors, in the cellar. Hanging them outdoors on Good Friday, she said, would ensure that the *Polizei* would come, ordering us to take them down. I hoped she was joking.

We went to a communion party. Along with the other eight-year-olds in the village, Marlene Hoenig celebrated her first communion. Such preparations all week long! Nelly cooked, baked, and cleaned the house from top to bottom while Marlene studied in church.

Then the out-of-town relatives came. We would see them walking up the road from the railroad station, carrying suitcases and wearing their Sunday best.

On the big day, the furniture was moved against the wall, table extensions were added, sparkling white cloths spread, and soon a proud table laid with china, crystal, and flowers stood dressed and waiting. At noon we went downstairs to join the other guests and never came up again until ten o'clock that night. Shy Marlene was flushed with excitement as she posed for Alan's camera.

After an afternoon of feasting, we started in with a six o'clock dinner meal. The food was amazing. Endless amounts of roasts and vegetables, breads and wine, cookies and cakes. Nelly had baked ten cakes herself, all of which were arrayed on her bed in anticipation of the dessert course.

A highlight of the occasion was a harmonica duet by Peter and Willi, the successful culmination of almost nightly rehearsal. There was a good deal of affectionate teasing of one elderly aunt. Tante Lena, sitting stiffly in her black suit with white, ruffled, high-necked blouse, agreed with one and all that she never drank, all the while downing one glass of sherry after another.

The arrival of a new baby is always cause for excitement. One day a neighbor rushed over, asking to use our phone so that she could call the prospective father, an American GI. He needed to come *"schnell"* as the baby was coming even "schneller." Then the midwife came running and there proceeded to be much activity back and forth to the stream, filling bucket after bucket of water. An hour or so later, a healthy baby boy had been born, and we heard that mother and son were doing just fine. We also heard that mother and father were definitely considering marriage.

Hexennacht, or the Night of the Witch, entranced the local children, including ours. Like Halloween, it took place in October, and like Halloween it had a connection to witches. But instead of the American observance with candy and costumes, the German children celebrated with fire and ritual.

The object of *Hexennacht* was to rid the community of all hexes and witches. For days the children gathered pieces of wood, trash, and whatever they could find to build bonfires. Then on the night of the great event, we all gathered in the field before the burning pyres. The children dipped torches into the flames, ignited them, and then waved them about to ward off any errant spirits that might be lurking about. Naturally, Alan and I were terrified; Peter and Steven were ecstatic.

We took the boys to Friday night services to celebrate the Sabbath with the other twenty-six American Jews stationed in the area. We had to come to Germany, it would seem, in order to find our way to prayer as Jews. For Rosh Hashanah services we drove fifty miles to Ramstein, the Air Force base, where Alan and I enjoyed it more than any time since childhood.

We felt the sound of the *shofar*, that solemn piping cry of the ages. We acutely felt the chanting of the rabbi, and as we joined in with the congregation reciting in unison we felt a connection with Jews everywhere.

Peter began first grade at the Air Force school in Birkenfeld. Steven, alone for the first time in his life, decided, as a tribute and as a salve to being left out of the momentous occasion, that he would follow suit (literally) as well. He got all dressed up and observed the whole day at home with me dressed up in school clothes, only changing into play clothes when Peter came home and did the same.

In the autumn, when the crops and the hay were in, the fields, which had been off-limits to the children became playgrounds once again. The boys were out there with their canteens hooked to their belts. Steven had a wooden toy wheelbarrow, and Peter never left home without his harmonica in his back pocket.

How wonderful to have a visit from home. How good that it was my mother. Returning from London with her we found the boys sitting on the stairs, ready to explode with anticipation. "Mommy! Daddy! Grandma!"

Everyone was talking at once, hugging and grabbing. Nelly reported in, stating that "the *Kinder* were very good." Rita and Marlene weighed in with "we played very much with Peter and Steven." And Anna silently and resolutely bent over to pick up clothing and a variety of other objects strewn about the floor.

Anna was upset. Certainly she wanted everything to be right for "the grandma." But for someone who felt as though *she* were the grandma, her subdued manner, a clear departure from her usual explosive demeanor, was a dead giveaway of her feelings of displacement.

She gave us a quick run-down of the children's activities during our absence: "Peter goes to school every day; he likes not to go to sleep at night. Steven plays with Hans Werner; he does not eat all his supper. We all go for walks to the *Gasthaus*; I take Katie; she is good, *immer gute.*"

The Katie. We all gathered around her crib as she opened her eyes to look at her grandma for the first time. It was love at first sight.

With Mother we visited castles in Heidelburg and the *Spielbank* (casino) in Wiesbaden. We took her to the Roman ruins in Trier and the Officer's Club at the 98th General Hospital. We drove to the PX in Baumholder and to a sausage festival in neighboring St. Wendel. There was dinner at the Yurichs' in Nohfelden and afternoon coffee with Nelly, where she and Mother exchanged recipes for potato pancakes (latkes), finding their respective Yiddish and German recipes were identical.

On the last day of Mother's stay she awoke early to find her grandsons already up, sadly aware that she was leaving. They spent a quiet hour alone together and then the baby, as if she too knew that she must be part of this, woke up so that the four of them could have their special time together before the whole household was up and about.

We stood on the railroad platform at Saarbrucken, waving goodbye to Mother as her train headed for Paris and home. We waved until we couldn't see her anymore, and then slowly, we turned away from the bright lights of Paris, home, and family, and headed back to Weiersbach.

It rained so much there. Too many days of gray. On one such day, as Anna and I sat together mending clothes while the children played at our feet and the rain pounded on the window, I started to speak with her about the war. All her bluster and ebullience seemed suddenly to evaporate.

She looked away, out through the rain-soaked window, and said, "All the Brown Shirts were bad." She was silent for a few minutes, and the only sound was the click of the plastic Lego pieces as Steven pressed them together to build a schoolhouse. Then Anna spoke again, remembering and recounting the past.

In 1939, she said, her father, already an old man set in his ways, thought it idiocy to be required to raise one's hand in the Nazi salute when greeting one's neighbors. His refusal to do so cost him. He was put on report by the *Burgermeister*, an active Gestapo man. Shipped off to jail for one hundred days, Anna's father, Herr Kirsch, served yet another jail term. The offense? He had remarked to a friend something to the effect that "Yes, indeed, it does appear that the Americans are going to win the war...."

Herr Kirsch is gone now, dead for many years. But the *Burgermeister* is still here. He rocks slowly back and forth on his porch, watching as we walk by on our strolls. We watch him too.

Holidays. Chanukah, Christmas, and St. Martin's Day. Village life for us had evolved to include customs new to us but centuries old. How strange it was to participate in customs previously unknown to us and quite foreign to our own cultural heritage. Yet there in Weiersbach the strange became commonplace.

Many centuries ago a gentle soul named Martin gave his cloak to a beggar, an act for which he is honored as St. Martin. The children of the village form a procession in the evening, marching through the streets and carrying lanterns in memory of the good St. Martin. Peter and Steven Rothstein marched too, unaware of any religious significance, happy to be part of the trail of lights bobbing gallantly through the darkening night.

The wheelbarrow race in Hoppstadten, the next town, was a very big deal. This was the event we had all been waiting for. Actually, some of us (including me) weren't really as enthusiastic as we might be.

I tried to get into the spirit of this thing, turning out with all the other village folk to watch the entrants run up and down the town square with empty wheelbarrows, baby buggies, anything on wheels, to determine who had the fastest wheelbarrow in the West—West Germany, that is.

Anna could almost have qualified for the race. She had fashioned a homemade vehicle perfect for transporting "the Katie" from room to room. All it was lacking was wheels. Anna took a large carton and cut a hole in the top, through which she lashed a rope. Now wherever Anna went, Katie went too.

The baby sat in the box happily playing while Anna folded laundry in the living room. Then when it was time to go to the kitchen to put on the kettle for afternoon tea, a journey of about thirty steps, Anna strode with baby and box in tow. Katie seemed to enjoy these little excursions, sucking her thumb and grinning at the passing hallway scenery. Katie was becoming bilingual. She could wave bye-bye in two languages. Anna said, "ata-ata" and Katie waved. We said "bye-bye" and she waved. Brilliant child.

We went to a birthday party. As the sole guests at Anna's birthday, we appeared at the appointed hour of four o'clock. A beaming Anna received us at her apartment. She lived in a single room furnished with stove and bed, wardrobe and table, and personal keepsakes everywhere. She poured coffee for us and served five cakes.

She was really feeling proud. Rudolf had called to wish his mother a happy birthday and to apologize for her present not being quite ready. Somehow her Christmas present was not quite ready either. But today, *"es macht nicht."* It matters not. Nothing could spoil Anna's celebration. She joyfully poured second cups of coffee for Peter and Steven, she cooed blissfully when Katie reached out for handfuls of cake, and she grabbed Alan and me in bear-hugs of kisses and tears, thanking us for our gift.

It is Mardi Gras or Carneval in other places; in Germany it is called Fasching. With it comes an endless array of festivities, music, beer, and hilarity. We went to a Fasching party with Nelly and Willi, where Alan and I were the only Americans. There were comedy skits presented at the local *Gasthaus*, and though we certainly missed some of the finer, untranslatable points of the skits, you didn't have to know German to be able to pick out the false noses and pie-in-the-face brand of comedy.

On the last day of Fasching we took the boys to Kaiserslautern, hoping to buy a magic set at the toy shop. But all the stores were closed. The city was completely given over to celebrants in the terminal stage of Fasching. There was a bus driver maneuvering his heavy, packed vehicle while sporting a putty nose and false mustache. There in the middle of the street sat a group of teenagers, singing and swaying. Everywhere people in costumes careened through the streets, still dressed up from the night before.

Katie's first birthday. Anna came bustling up to the house early in the morning like something out of *Alice in Wonderland*. "It isn't ready," she sputtered, "it isn't ready; it was supposed to be ready." She then went away as quickly as she had come, only to return a bit later. This time with a triumphant glint in her eye, she charged up the stairs, stopping to catch her breath. "Here!" she said as she thrust an enormous package into my arms.

I was holding a bolt of beautiful velvet cloth and listening as Anna gave me my instructions. "You must bring the velvet to Frau Hollander and have a dress and coat made up for Katie." With bemused but genuine thanks, I accepted the lovely gift on behalf of the little girl who was at that moment sound asleep in a wet diaper and a blue striped hand-me-down shirt of her brother Steven's.

In the evening, all of Katie's devoted subjects—Alan and I, Peter and Steven, Nelly and Willi, Rita and Marlene and Anna and Rudolf—celebrated with birthday cake. From the vantage point of her high-chair throne, Katie posed for pictures, clapped her hands, and ate her cake. She also wore it all over her dress. It was a lovely time.

Alan made his debut as guest lecturer when the rabbi invited him to speak at the Purim services. Reluctant though he was, he agreed to do it, with the proviso that I help him write it. His topic was "A Psychiatrist Looks at Prejudice." In one evening he was able to dispel, for many people, the impressions of a formidable, forbidding authority figure, the psychiatrist. Relaxed and funny, he captivated his audience.

Then, to everyone's displeasure, two noisy children at the back of the hall created a disturbance. When the annoyance did not abate, Alan remarked that it was perhaps understandable how intolerance could grow, as he was himself "beginning to develop a healthy prejudice against small children." Everyone laughed and applauded, and we heard no more from the back of the hall.

A trip to town was always a novelty for us village people. In Idar-Oberstein, one could peer in shop windows at beautiful handmade wooden toys or luscious-looking pastries, or one could inch along a sidewalk so narrow pedestrians had to walk single-file.

On one particular day, we were just emerging from a department store when we were surprised by rumbling sounds coming down the cobblestone street. Then a convoy of tanks and armored trucks appeared, and people began to stream out of the shops and gather along the sidewalks. They were exhilarated by the sight of the young men manning the machines of the new German Army.

Children waved and jumped up and down, thrilled at the sight of real-life war games, as the young soldiers headed out on maneuvers. The people called out greetings and well wishes to the passing troops. Alan and I, however, stood silently rooted to the sidewalk as all around us cheers rose for the gladiators. And then they were gone. People slowly filtered back into the shops and moved along the streets chatting softly as Volkswagens and motorbikes crawled through the winding streets honking their horns.

All had quickly returned to normal. No longer was there any army to cheer—or fear. Only everyday people going about their daily business, buying bread, perhaps a pound or two of bratwurst, pricing the linen dresses on display in the window, and then going home to a good hot meal with the family, which is what we did, albeit in a more somber and sober mood than before.

The bleak Nahe valley, our home these two years, seemed always gray. But occasionally there was a fine day, and a walk through the woods over millions of brittle pine needles underfoot felt like a splendid adventure. Katie was a bundle of chirping delight as she reached up for the pieces of sun filtering through the treetops.

And then we were just a month away from going home. As wonderful as it was for us, it was awful for Anna. We tried to pretend it wasn't happening, and then, of course, something would come up in casual conversation and she was up and out of the room, the hem of her apron pulled up as she dabbed at her eyes, the tears spilling down her face.

On our last evening with Nelly and Willi we drank a toast to friendship, but Nelly, with her fear of flying, said, "I'll only come to see you in America when they build a bridge!" Peter and Steven excitedly described to Rita and Marlene how they would soon be flying over the ocean in a b-i-g airplane, only to be stopped short with bewilderment as the girls burst into tears and fled the room.

We had a last dinner at the Officers' Club with acquaintances who themselves would soon be heading back to New York, California, and points between. We also had a last dinner with the Yurichs as we recounted our experiences: "Remember the day we all arrived? All eight of us—two of us pregnant!—piling into that borrowed Chevy for a three-hour ride to a place called Weiersbach? Remember all the times the *Burgermeister* shut off the water? How about the time they found the bomb under the bridge? Remember the *Swartz Mann* and *Hexennacht* and Sunday strolls by honeypiles, and always the rain...remember?

We remembered. But most of all we remembered Anna. We won't forget the last forlorn weeks leading up to the final farewell. Anna blowing her nose loudly into a dampened handkerchief, chin trembling. It was impossible to soothe her, impossible to comfort her, impossible to forget her.

In years to come, when I think of Germany I will think of that gray valley along the Nahe River, of castles on the Rhine, of vineyards along the Mosel. I will recall the chimneysweep and the bakery truck and a sleigh ride in Berchtesgarten. I will remember an old man in a rocking chair who used to wear the uniform of the Gestapo.

I will recall the many music festivals and Fasching festivals, sausage festivals and "festival festivals." I will remember the Frankfurt Zoo and the vitality of West Berlin and the grimness of east Berlin. I'll remember a boat ride along the Rhine, the passion play at Oberamergau and the horror that was Dachau.

I will think of the little town of Idar-Oberstein, where there is a thriving business in semiprecious stones and where all the former Jewish practitioners of that craft are now gone. I will think of the Hoenigs, Nelly, Willi, Marlene and Rita, and of their kindness, their decency, and their friendship.

But mostly, I think, I will remember Anna. Anna with the wide grin and open arms. Anna who tore the sheets and mended the socks, who clattered in the kitchen and crooned to a baby. Anna who spilled the soup and soothed a little boy with a scraped knee. Anna who gave and gave and never held back. Anna who could act as giddy and giggly as a schoolgirl and as old as Methuselah. Anna who put a human face, a personal stamp, on a place that still did—and always would—resonate with the Shoah, the Holocaust. I will never forget Anna. *Immer* Anna.

XXIV. Rite of Passage

When the time comes for you to live, there aren't enough years.

—*Jewish Proverb*

MY FATHER DIED IN 1973, at the age of seventy-five. My mother's death occurred just a year later; she was only seventy-four.

They were children of immigrant parents, not born to comfort or security. And they and their contemporaries gave birth to American children, children who never knew anything but comfort and security. In the space of two generations, an American family, with all its privilege and opportunity, had emerged.

My parents, Frank and Frances Manson, forged the link from the Old World to the new. Their lives began in Boston among other immigrant families, where there were limited resources yet unlimited hopes. At the time of their deaths, my parents had shared more than forty years of marriage, experienced a Depression, the struggle for financial security, the loss of parents and siblings, my mother's bouts with colon cancer and heart disease, and my father's diabetes and strokes. And through it all they found joy in their family.

At my father's funeral, at the graveside, I read these words:

"My father, Frank Manson was born in 1898 in Boston, lived here all of his life, and died in May 1973, at the age of seventy-five. Before the onset of his first illness, a stroke in 1966, my father had known complete good health and had possessed a vigorous and spirited nature.

"Throughout the last seven years of his life, with the onslaught of repeated strokes and illnesses, he still retained his sense of humor, his dignity and his spirit.

"My father worked most of his life as a salesman; he enjoyed meeting people and was very successful and at ease in his work, as he was in his life. He was an uncomplicated man whose life and happiness centered on home, family, and friends.

"As for religion, while he did not practice orthodoxy in his religious life, he maintained the precepts and principles of Judaism, and he celebrated the holidays with great dedication.

"My father was devoted to my mother, adoring of me, his only child, enormously proud of his son-in-law, and head-over-heels in love with his grandchildren. We all loved him and will miss him."

Thirteen months later, my mother, Frances Manson, was gone too. Unlike my father, she had a complicated nature. Also unlike my father, who was not overly ambitious, my mother wanted more than she got. More children, more recognition, more respect, more.

Fannie was the only one of ten siblings who took an aged mother, my grandmother Jennie, into her home. It was Fannie who, as a girl, sewed a party dress for herself and was startled when her sister Bessie skipped off to a dance wearing it. It was Fannie who wanted to be called Frances, but who never was.

My mother was the dutiful one who wanted to be lighthearted but wasn't. She was kind and loving, practical and earnest. She didn't always understand the jokes that others told. She was cautious and protective, and I didn't always understand that.

In her middle years she started smoking. Not well, and not for long. She also went back to work part-time. She hired herself out as a temp, a temporary secretary, working only when she wanted to, for the times when she wanted money for something special, something apart from family finances. She earned the money herself, for example, to finance a trip to Germany to visit us and meet her infant granddaughter for the first time.

In addition to the loss of my parents, their deaths represented a rite of passage for me, one that somehow took me by surprise. Always my parents, my aunts and uncles, and others had been there; they were, after all, the older generation. Now they were gone, and for what it was worth, I was "the older generation." Now Alan and I would be the ones to conduct the Passover seder; no more would I listen to my father intone the prayers or watch him sip his ceremonial wine from the ruby red glass inscribed "Frankie, 1908."

Now it was our turn to shepherd growing children through trials and challenges. The next time we would hear the words "Grandma and Grandpa" they would refer to us. To inherit the mantle of the older generation was in the natural order of things, but nonetheless a shock. Today, as Alan and I head up a three-generation family of fourteen, it is a thrill, and still a shock.

I think of us, my children, and my grandchildren, as part of a long line that originated in the *stetlach* of Eastern Europe from a people who were, among other things, survivors.

Our ancestors dreamed of a future in which their children might prosper and be safe. Beyond the harshness of daily life, they must have also hoped for some joy, some happiness. Their hopes and dreams became our inheritance. Our lives are a testament to their tenacity, to their struggle for a "better life" for their children and their children's children. Though each generation has its own struggles and dreams, for me and my family, as well as for many another family of immigrants, the hopes of my people have come true in America.

Epilogue

THE BOOK IS AT AN END, but the story goes on. Future generations will write their own chapters. And the past may yield further secrets as new archival records appear from Eastern Europe, bringing data that may enlighten and inform.

Much has been uncovered already. Records from Belarus and Lithuania have introduced me to my grandfather's siblings. I wish my mother could have known that her father, Wolf Frumkin, had a sister named Devorah.

My mother did know her uncle Morris Frumkin, who also emigrated to Boston. But I don't believe she knew about her Ohio relatives. I only discovered them recently through a contact in "The Jewish Family Finder," a sort of bulletin-board publication for those seeking family connections. That is how I found Mark Teitlebaum.

Mark is the same age as my son Peter; in fact, he heads a family just like mine, in which he is the eldest of three with a younger brother and sister born the same years as my son Steven and my daughter Katie. Mark is a descendant of Abraham Mendel Frumkin, and the information we were able to share has filled in blank spaces in both our family genealogies.

On the Movschovitz/Manson side of the family, with the aid of records now available from Vilnius, I found that my Grandfather Harris was the only son and the eldest of four. Prior to that I had no knowledge of his siblings. I was also able to learn about his being drafted into the army of the czar in the year 1880, when he was nineteen.

"Enlisted" in the local unit of the National Guard is how the Lithuanian archival information describes Grandpa's conscription. He had to report for duty in Trakei, a few miles south of his town of Yanova and only eighteen miles out of Vilnius. There is no record of whether or not he actually went to Trakei.

But I was there. Traveling through Lithuania in search of roots, we went to this small resort town without knowing that it had served as the draft board in my grandfather's day. We went to see Trakei's fourteenth-century castle, a tourist attraction that surely would not have been on Grandpa's itinerary.

Trying to bring the family records up to date has resulted in many hours of research and phone calls. I have found cousins still living in the Boston area and contacted others at their current homes in California, Florida, and Texas. And I was thrilled to locate my cousin Richard Franklin, long missing from the family circle. Through the Internet I was able to trace him to Switzerland, where he has lived for the last twenty-five years. We are currently very busy getting to know each other again.

I had a wonderful day in New Jersey at the lovely lakeside home of my cousin Kenneth Barton, getting acquainted with him, his wife, Charni, and his mother, Natalie. Ken's father, Harold, was my first cousin, but I never knew him. A casualty of World War II, he died leaving his wife and four-year-old Ken.

We told stories that day, stories of remembrance, of Ken's Nana Betty, my mother's sister, and of other relations who have touched our lives. Ken told of his undergraduate education at NYU, much of which was financed by a "death benefit" from his father. Was there ever a more awful oxymoron than that?

After graduation, Ken worked for a time as a stevedore as he made his way through dental school. Today he is a successful orthodontist.

It is telling in the extreme to note that from the ten Franklin siblings, only eleven children were born. We are first cousins whose birth years span more than thirty years, beginning in 1913 and ending in 1945 with the conclusion of World War II.

On my father's side, the Movschovitz/Manson side, there were six siblings who lived to adulthood. As one of the eight children born to them, it seemed to me, as I was growing up, that I had lots of family, *mishpocheh*. But the fact is, my mother's words "it was the Depression" carried deeper meaning as to why the Mansons, the Franklins, and others of that generation had so few children. They simply couldn't afford them.

And it was something else, too. Having grown up with so little and having to share what little there was with so many, my parents and their contemporaries found they did not have much desire to replicate those conditions.

For me it may have been picturesque and amusing to conjure up the vision of my Aunt Helen, the youngest of the ten Franklin children, sleeping in a bureau drawer, the only space for an infant in an overcrowded household. But maybe it wasn't picturesque, and probably it wasn't amusing. It may just have been difficult.

The people I come from, while proudly Jewish, were not profoundly so. They were casual practitioners of their religion. We went to synagogue on the High Holidays, fasted on Yom Kippur, and brought out the Menorah from its year-long hiding place in order to light the Chanukah candles. We donated money to plant trees in Israel.

As for me, though my cultural and ethnic ties with Judaism are stronger than ever, I cannot claim to have become more religious through the writing of this book. I still only go to synagogue on the High Holidays.

But I am drawn to synagogues wherever I go. As a result, I have been to a Bar Mitzvah in Izmir, Turkey, and to a wedding at a kibbutz in Israel. I have donned a scarf and climbed the stairs to the women's section of an Orthodox synagogue in Moscow. In Minsk and Vilnius and Kaunas I have seen what is left of once-vital Jewish communities and visited the single remaining synagogue in each of those cities.

In Warsaw, Alan and I visited the ghetto and the one remaining synagogue, a place of worship that had been used as a stable by the Nazis during World War II. In Turkey we had to show identification to armed guards in order to gain entry to the *shul*. In Costa Rica the synagogue was closed and guarded by armed militia. In Nairobi, Kenya, the caretaker had to unlock the gate so that we could enter the synagogue: a small, white-washed, single-story building.

Today we Jews, descendants of Abraham, Jacob, and Isaac, of Sarah, Ruth, and Naomi, still roam the world. But for most of us, particularly for American Jews, it is a voluntary wandering, impelled not by force and necessity but by desire.

I am grateful that I have had a chance to tell this story and grateful for what I discovered on the way. I found new family members along with old family connections. I discovered that I cared more than I realized about things that symbolized those connections. My mother's china cups and saucers, which I either ignored or disdained as I was growing up in her house, are now treasured objects in my house.

I found that remembering my father, his sweetness, his spirit, and his teasing humor, all of which his grandson Steven inherited, made me glad and grateful.

I found out how much I was connected to my mother by our natures and our interests. More than I had known. Like her I am a person who makes lists and remembers to send out birthday cards and thank-you notes. Like her, I am the family historian.

And like my mother I think that I take more risks now than I did when I was younger. She was in her late forties when she took driving lessons. It wasn't until I was forty that I returned to work or published any of my writing. This spring I am taking flying lessons.

In writing this book I felt as if I was taking a huge risk. Could I do it? Once I had embarked on the project, I would have to see it through to the end. What made me think that I was an historian?

I recalled the words writer Dorothy Parker used when she heard herself compared to poet Edna St. Vincent Millay. Parker remarked that she might be following in the footsteps of the great Millay, "but unfortunately in my own ugly sneakers."

I understood that. But I also understood that if I laced up those "ugly sneakers" every morning and went to work, I'd get to where I was going. As Woody Allen says, "Ninety percent of life is showing up."

The words of other writers frequently come to me, to comfort, to amuse, to inspire. It is Robert Frost I think of now. In writing this book, with its flaws and limitations, I chose a path, one that was often lonely and uncertain. But it turned out to be "the road less traveled by, and that has made all the difference."

Suggested Reading

Allen, Frederick Lewis. *Only Yesterday*. New York: Harper & Brothers, 1932.

——. *Since Yesterday*. New York: Bantam Books, 1961.

Angoff, Charles. *When I Was a Boy in Boston*. New York: Beechhurst Press, 1947.

Antin, Mary. *From Plotzk to Boston*. New York: Marcus Wiener Publishing, Inc., 1985 (originally published 1899).

——*The Promised Land*. Boston: Houghton Mifflin Co., 1969 (originally published 1912).

Aronson, Chaim. *A Jewish Life Under the Tsars*. New York: Allanheld, Osmun & Co., 1983.

Ausubel, Nathan. (Updated by David C. Gross). *Pictorial History of the Jewish People*. New York: Crown Publishers, Inc., 1953, 1984.

Bailey, Ronald H. and the Editors of Time-Life Books. *The Home Front: U.S.A.* New Jersey: Time-Life Books, Inc., 1977.

Baron, Joseph Louis. *A Treasury of Jewish Quotations*. New York: J. Aronson, 1985.

Baron, Salo W. *The Russian Jew Under Tsars and Soviets*. New York: Macmillan Co., 1964, 1976.

Bernstein, Burton. *Family Matters, Sam, Jennie and the Kids*. New York: Summit Books, 1982.

Birmingham, Stephen. *The Rest of Us, the Rise of America's Eastern European Jews*. Boston, Toronto: Little, Brown & Co., 1984.

——. *Black Book of Localities Whose Jewish Population Was Exterminated by the Nazis.* Yad Vashem, Jerusalem: Martyrs' and Heroes' Remembrance Authority, 1965.

Blumenthal, Shirley. *Coming to America.* New York: Delacorte Press, 1981.

Brodie, Deborah, ed. *Stories My Grandfather Should Have Told Me.* New York, London: Bonim Books, 1977.

Broner, E.M. *The Telling.* New York: Harper Collins, 1983.

Brownstone, David M. *The Jewish-American Heritage.* New York: Facts on File Publications, 1988.

Brownstone, David M., Franck, Irene M. and Brownstone, Douglass L. *Island of Hope, Island of Tears.* New York: Rawson, Wade Publishers, Inc., 1979.

Burstein, Chaya M. *The Jewish Kids Catalogue.* Philadelphia: Jewish Publishing Society of America, 1983.

Butwin, Frances. *The Jews in America.* Minnesota: Lerner Publishing Co., 1969.

Cahan, Abrahm. *The Rise of David Levinsky.* Gloucester, MA: Peter Smith, 1969 (originally published by Harper & Brothers, 1917).

Chagal, Bella. *Burning Lights.* New York: Schocken Books, 1946.

Chermayeff, Ivan; Wasserman, Fred and Shapiro, Mary. *Ellis Island.* New York: Macmillan Publishing Company, 1991.

Chernin, Kim. *In My Mother's House.* New Haven, Ct.: Ticknor & Fields, 1983.

Cohen, Chester G. *Shtetl Finder: Jewish Communities in the 19th and 20th Centuries in the Pale of the Settlement of Russia and Poland, and in Lithuania, Latvia, Galicia and Bukovina.* Los Angeles: Periday Co., 1980.

Coletta, John P. *They Came in Ships.* Salt Lake City: Ancestry, 1989.

Dawidowicz, Lucy S. *The Golden Tradition.* New York: Holt, Rinehart & Winston, 1967.

Dershowitz, Alan M. *Chutzpah.* Boston, Toronto, London: Little, Brown & Co., 1991.

Dimont, Max. *Jews, God and History*. New York: Simon and Schuster, 1962.

Dimont, Max I. *The Jews in America*. New York: Touchstone Books, Simon and Schuster, 1978.

Eban, Abba. *Heritage: Civilization and the Jews*. New York: Summit Books, 1984.

———. *Encyclopedia Judaica*. New York: The Macmillan Company, 1971.

Fein, Isaac M. *Boston—Where It All Began, An Historical Perspective of the Boston Jewish Community*. Boston: Boston Jewish Bicentennial Comm., 1976.

Frank, Anne. *The Diary of a Young Girl*. Garden City, New York: Doubleday & Company, Inc., 1967

Franklin, Sidney. *Bullfighter from Brooklyn*. Prentice-Hall, Inc., 1952.

Gittleman, Sol. *From Shtetl to Suburbia*. Boston: Beacon Press, 1978.

Goodman, Henry, ed. *The New Country*. New York: Ykuf Publishers, 1961.

Gordon, Albert I. *Jews in Suburbia*. Boston: Beacon Press, 1959.

Gross, David C. and Gross, Esther R. *Jewish Wisdom, A Treasury of Proverbs, Maxims, Aphorisms, Wise Sayings, and Memorable Quotations*. New York: Walker and Company, 1992.

Hacker, Tina, ed. *Shalom*. Kansas City: Hallmark Cards, Inc., 1972.

Halberstam, David. *The Fifties*. New York: Villard Books, 1993.

Handlin, Oscar. *Adventure in Freedom*. New York: McGraw-Hill Book Company, Inc., 1954.

———*Boston's Immigrants*. Cambridge, MA: Belknap Press of Harvard University Press, 1981 (originally published in 1941).

———*A Pictorial History of Immigration*. New York: Crown Publishers, Inc., 1972.

———*The Uprooted*. New York: Grosset & Dunlap, 1951.

Hapgood, Hutchins. *The Spirit of the Ghetto*. Cambridge, MA: Belknap Press of Harvard University Press, 1967 (originally published in 1902).

Hentoff, Nat. *Boston Boy*. New York: Alfred A. Knopf, 1986.

Hoffman, Eva. *Lost in Translation*. New York: Penguin Books, 1989.

Howe, Irving. *The World of Our Fathers*. New York: Harcourt Brace Jovanovich, 1976.

——and Libo, Kenneth. *How We Lived: A Documentary History of Immigrant Jews in America*. New York: New American Library, 1979.

——and Wisse, Ruth R., ed. *The Best of Sholom Aleichem*. New York: Touchstone Book, Simon & Schuster, 1980.

Hubmann, Franz. *The Jewish Family Album*. Boston: Little, Brown and Company. 1974.

——. *Jewish Encyclopedia*. New York and London: Funk and Wagnalls Co., 1903.

Israel, Sherry. *Boston's Jewish Community*. [The 1985 CJP Demographic Study] Boston: Combined Jewish Philanthropies, 1987.

Karp, Abraham, ed. *Golden Door to America*. New York: Viking Press, 1976.

Kazin, Alfred. *New York Jew*. New York: Alfred A. Knopf, Inc., 1978.

Kogos, Fred. *1001 Yiddish Proverbs*. New York: Carol Publishing Group, 1990.

Kramer, Sydelle and Masur, Jenny. *Jewish Grandmothers*. Boston: Beacon Press, 1976.

Kugelmass, Jack and Boyarin, Jonathan. *From a Ruined Garden, The Memorial Books of Polish Jewry*. New York: Schocken Books, 1983.

Landau, Ron. *The Book of Jewish Lists*. New York: Stein and Day, 1982.

Lazowski, Rabbi Philip. *A Passover Haggadah: From the Depths of Redemption*.

Lerman, Antony, ed. *The Jewish Communities of the World*. New York: Facts on File, Inc., 1989.

Levitan, Tina. *Jews in American Life from 1492 to the Space Age*. New York: Hebrew Publishing Co., 1969.

Levine, Hillel and Harman, Lawrence. *The Death of an American Jewish Community, A Tragedy of Good Intentions*. New York: The Free Press, A Division of Macmillan, Inc., 1992.

Linfield, Harry S. *The Jews in the United States, 1927. A Study of Their Number and Distribution.* New York: The American Jewish Committee, 1929.

Lingeman, Richard R. *Don't You Know There's A War On?, The American Home Front, 1941–1945.* New York: G.P. Putnam's Sons, 1970.

Lukas, J. Anthony. *Common Ground.* New York: Vintage Books, 1986.

Manners, Ande. *Poor Cousins.* New York: Coward, McCann and Geoghegan, Inc., 1972.

Markowitz, Rabbi Sidney L. *What You Should Know About Jewish Religion, History, Ethics, and Culture.* New York: The Citadel Press, 1955.

Melamed, Frances. *Janova.* Cincinnati, Ohio: Janova Press, Inc., 1976.

Meltzer, Milton. *Remember the Days.* Garden City, NY: Zenith Books, Doubleday and Co., Inc., 1974.

——. *World of Our Fathers.* New York: Farrar, Strauss and Giroux, 1974.

Metzger, Isaac. *A Bintel Brief.* New York: Doubleday and Co., Inc., 1971.

Miller, Arthur. *Timebends: A Life.* New York: Grove Press, 1987.

Morrison, Joan and Zabusky, Charlotte Fox. *American Mosaic. The Immigrant Experience in the Words of Those Who Lived It.* New York: E.P. Dutton, 1980.

Mokotoff, Gary and Sack, Sallyann Amdur. *Where Once We Walked: A Guide to the Jewish Communities Destroyed in the Holocaust.* Teaneck, NJ: Avotaynu, Inc., 1991.

Muggamin, Howard. *The Jewish Americans [The Peoples of North America].* New York and Philadelphia: Chelsea House Publishers, 1988.

Neugroschel, Joachim, ed. *The Shtetl, A Creative Anthology of Jewish Life in Eastern Europe.* New York: Richard Marek Publishers, 1979.

Novotny, Ann. *Strangers at the Door. (Ellis Island, Castle Garden and the Great Migration to America.)* Riverside, CT: The Chatham Press, Inc., 1971.

——*On Common Ground, The Boston Jewish Experience, 1649–1980.* American Jewish Historical Society, 1981.

Perlmutter, Nathan and Perlmutter, Ruth Ann. *The Real Anti-Semitism in America.* New York: Arbor House, 1982.

Peter, Dr. Laurence J. *Peter's Quotations*. Bantam Books, 1977.

Phillips, Bruce A. *Acculturation, Group Survival and the Ethnic Communities: A Social History of the Jewish Community of Brookline, Massachusetts 1915–1940*. UCLA [dissertation], 1975.

——*Brookline: the Evolution of an American Jewish Suburb*. [From a series titled European Immigrants and American Society] New York and London: Garland Publishing, Inc., 1990.

Peichotka, Maria and Kazimierz. *Wooden Synagogues*. Warsaw: Arkady, 1959.

Roiphe, Anne. *Generation Without Memory, A Jewish Journey in Christian America*. New York: Linden Press/Simon and Schuster, 1981.

Roskies, Diane. *The Shtetl Book*. New York: Ktav Publishers, 1975.

Rosten, Leo. *Hooray For Yiddish*. New York: A Touchstone Book, Simon & Schuster, Inc., 1982.

——. *The Joys of Yiddish*. New York: McGraw-Hill, 1968.

——. *The Joys of Yinglish*. New York: McGraw-Hill, 1989.

Roth, Henry. *Call It Sleep*. New York: Cooper Square Publishers, 1965 (originally published 1934).

Roth, Philip. *The Facts: A Novelist's Autobiography*. New York: Farrar, Strauss and Giroux, Inc., 1988.

Rottenberg, Dan. *Finding Our Fathers, A Guidebook to Jewish Genealogy*. New York: Random House, 1977.

Rubin, Steven J., ed. *Writing Our Lives: Autobiographies of American Jews, 1890–1990*. Philadelphia, New York, Jerusalem: The Jewish Publication Society, 1991.

Runes, Dagobert D. *Dictionary of Judaism*. New York: The Wisdom Library, a division of Philosophical Library, 1959.

——. *Jewish Proverbs*. San Francisco: Chronicle Books, 1989.

Sachar, Abram. *A History of the Jews*. New York: Alfred A. Knopf, 1965 (5th edition).

Sack, Sallyann Amdur. *A Guide to Jewish Genealogical Research in Israel*. Baltimore: Genealogical Publishing Co., 1987.

Samuel, Maurice. *The World of Sholom Aleichem*. New York: Schocken Books, 1965.

Sarna, Jonathan D. and Smith, Ellen; editors. *The Jews of Boston*. Boston: Combined Jewish Philanthropies of Greater Boston Inc., 1995.

Schoenberg, Nancy and Stuart. *Lithuanian Jewish Communities*. New York: Garland Publishing, 1991.

Schoener, Allon. *The American Jewish Album (1654 to the Present)*. New York: Rizzoli, 1983.

———ed. *Portal to America: the Lower East Side, 1870–1925*. New York, Chicago, San Francisco: Holt, Rinehart and Winston, 1967.

Shepard, Richard F. and Levi, Vicki Gold. *Live and Be Well, a Celebration of Yiddish Culture in America from the First Immigrants to the Second World War*. Worthington, MA: Hilltown Press, 1982.

Sholem Aleichem. *The Tevye Stories and Others*. New York: Pocket Books, 1965.

Shulman, Abraham. *The New Country*. New York: Charles Scribner's Sons, 1976.

———. *The Old Country*. New York: Charles Scribner's Sons, 1974.

Sklare, Marshall. *America's Jews*. New York: Random House, Inc., 1971.

Simon, Kate. *Bronx Primitive. Portraits in a Childhood*. New York: Viking Press, 1982.

Simons, Howard. *Jewish Times (Voices of the American Jewish Experience)*. Boston: Houghton Mifflin Co., 1988.

Singer, I.B. *Gimpel the Fool*. New York: Farrar. Strauss and Giroux, 1951.

———. *The Spinoza of Market Place*. New York: Farrar, Strauss and Giroux, 1951.

Singer, I.J. *The Brothers Ashkenazi*. New York: Alfred A. Knopf, 1933.

Thaden, Edward C. *Russia Since 1801: The Making of a New Society*. New York: Wiley-Interscience, 1971.

Tifft, Wilton and Dunne, Thomas. *Ellis Island*. New York: W.W. Norton and Company Inc., 1971.

This Fabulous Century. (Vol. III, 1920–1930; Vol. IV, 1930–1940). Alexandria, VA: Time-Life Books, 1969.

Van Den Haag, Ernest. *The Jewish Mystique*. New York: Stein and Day, 1969.

Warner, Sam B. *Streetcar Suburbs, The Process of Growth in Boston 1870–1900*. Cambridge, MA: Harvard University Press and the M.I.T. Press, 1962.

Weinberg, Sydney Stahl. *The World of Our Mothers, The Lives of Jewish Immigrant Women*. Chapel Hill and London: The University of North Carolina Press, 1988.

Wiesenthal, Simon. *Every Day Remembrance Day. A Chronicle of Jewish Martyrdom*. New York: Henry Holt and Company, 1986.

White, Theodore. *In Search of History, A Personal Adventure*. New York: Harper and Row, 1978.

Wirth, Louis. *The Ghetto*. Chicago: The University of Chicago Press, 1928 and 1956.

Zborowski, Mark and Herzog, Elizabeth. *Life Is with People: The Jewish Little-Town of Eastern Europe*. New York: International Universities Press, 1952.

Zubatsky, David S. and Berent, Irwin M. *Jewish Genealogy: A Sourcebook of Family Histories and Genealogies*. New York: Garland Publishing Co., 1983.